Contract Law

Review & Revision Study Guide

Mohammed Subhan Hussain

SULIS
ACADEMIC
PRESS

An Imprint of Sulis International
Los Angeles | London

CONTRACT LAW: REVIEW & REVISION STUDY GUIDE

Library of Congress Control Number: 2018945049
ISBN: 978-1-946849-26-7
eISBN: 978-1-946849-27-4

www.sulisinternational.com

Contents

1. Offer and Acceptance...1
2. Intention to Create Legal Relations 23
3. What is a Term? 28
4. The Sources of Contractual Terms..31
5. The Classification of Contractual Terms 65
6. Exclusion Clauses 77
7. Misrepresentation..113
8. Common Mistake and Frustration 138
9. Duress, Undue Influence, Inequality of Bargaining Power 171
10. Performance and Discharge of the Contract 188
11. Breach of Contract 191
12. Obtaining an Adequate Remedy 200
About the Author..224

1. Offer and Acceptance

Offer and Invitation to Treat

- **Offer** – a statement by a contracting party that they are willing to form a contract on the terms provided for within that statement. This offer can be stated orally, by the party's conduct or through a written offer. A contract is formed if an offer is accepted.

- **Invitation to treat** – an invitation to treat differs because the statement merely indicates a willingness to enter negotiations. An invitation to treat cannot be 'accepted' to form a contract.

Can distinguish between these two statements by looking at the intention of the party. Did they intend only to continue or enter negotiations or was their statement an indication that they wished to conclude a legal agreement? This distinction is not always clear.

Complexities when deciphering between an *offer* and *invitation to treat*

Ex. Gibson v Manchester City Council (1978)
Facts

- 1970 - defendant council sent a brochure explaining how a council tenant could purchase their council house, this was received by tenants who had said previously they wished to purchase a council house.

- The brochure contained a form to be filled in by those wishing to purchase their home.

- Mr Gibson filled in the form and returned it to the council.

- Council replied to inform him that the "council may be prepared to sell the house" to him at a stated price, and that if he wanted to make a "formal application" to buy the house, he should complete another form.

- Mr Gibson did this, but left purchase price blank, because he wanted to know whether the council would complete repairs to his house, or whether he would have to at a cost which he would seek to have reduced from the purchase price.

— The council replied clarifying the price included the need for repairs.

— Mr Gibson accepted this and requested the application continued. He subsequently paid for repairs.

— At this stage, Labour party won local elections and discontinued the policy of selling council houses. All sales were cancelled, except for those where a contract had already been formed.

— Mr Gibson's case was deemed to be one in which no contract had been concluded.

Judgement
Offer

— Trial judge and Court of Appeal - contract had been concluded.

— **Lord Denning** - agreement on all material points, despite formalities not being completed.

Not an offer

— **House of Lords** - no contract.

— Letter written by treasurer stating that the "council may be prepared to sell", was not an offer, it did not mean after obligations could be created merely because Mr Gibson agreed to purchase the house.

— It was merely a willingness to enter into negotiations for the sale of the house.

— Mr Gibson was invited to make a "formal application" to purchase the house and not to signify his agreement to the stated terms.

Complexities

- In a case such as Gibson, the court strives to find the intention of the parties, and whether they intended to make an offer.

- In cases such as advertisements and shop-window display - the courts are more concerned to establish clear rules.

- *Treitel* - "it may be possible to displace these rules by evidence of contrary intention, but in the absence of such evidence (these rules of law) will determine the distinction between offer and invitation to treat, and they will do so without reference to the intention (actual or even objectively ascertained) of the maker of the statement"

Display of goods for sale

3 approaches adopted to the display of goods for sale in a shop

1. **Display of goods is an offer, which is accepted when goods are picked up by purchaser.**

Undesirable consequences

- Purchaser bound as soon as they pick anything up.

- Would be in breach of contract if they subsequently changed their mind, or chose a different product.

1. **Display of goods is an offer, which is accepted when the purchaser takes goods to the cash desk**

This is undesirable, as consequences are that...

- Offer will take away the shopkeeper's freedom to bargain argument.

- However, it can be argued this does not represent reality. Most shops operate a 'take it or leave it policy'. No bargaining.

- Would a display and a purchaser bringing cash to the desk lead to a contract even when the shop's stocks had run out, and it was unable to actually provide the goods offered? (Partridge v Crittenden [1968]) This criticism can be levelled by implying that all displays as offers are dependent on supplies.

3

1. **The display of goods constitutes an invitation to treat that the offer is made by the purchaser when they bring the goods to the tills. At this point, the offer is accepted by the shopkeeper.**

– No rigidity of price for purchaser.

– Ex. Customer that takes goods to cash desk may be told that the goods are on sale for a higher price than the display price

– No way customer could compel shopkeeper to sells goods at the display price in a civil case.

– Seller may be subject to Criminal sanctions under the *Consumer Protection from Unfair Trading Regulations (2008)* for providing misleading details about prices. But this leaves no civil remedy for a purchaser.

Courts position
Display of goods in a shop window is an invitation to treat (Fisher v Bell 1961)
Ex. Pharmaceutical Society GB v Boots Cash Chemists (1953)
Facts

– Defendants utilised self-service in their shop.

– *Pharmacy and Poisons Act 1933 S18 (1)* - breach of this section if a sale of drugs take place without the supervision of a registered pharmacist.

– If a customer was accepting an offer by picking up items from the shelf without a pharmacist the shop would be breaching the section.

Judgement

– Held that sale took place at the cash desk.

– Display of goods was simply an invitation to treat

– no breach of the act

Complexities

The rule in Boots intuitively feels fair, the shop did have a registered pharmacist overseeing sales, to find them in breach of the act would be to neglect this.
Rigid application of rule can lead to injustice in some instances
Authority for treating displays as offers?
Ex. Chapleton v Barry (1940) **(Treating display goods as an offer)**

- Display of deck chairs for hire on a beach was an offer which was accepted by a customer taking a chair from the stack (see Carlill v Carbolic Smoke ball Co 1983)

- Like Boots, this feels intuitively fair. If the claimant had not concluded a contract when he took the chair, he would not have a remedy for the chairs breaking and his subsequent injury.

- This is an example of *"reasoning backwards" (Professor Atiyah)*

Advertisements

Newspaper advertisements is an invitation to treat, rather than an offer
Ex. Partridge v Crittenden (1968)
Facts

- Appellant advertised Bramblefinch cocks and hens for sale.

- Protection of Birds Act 1954 - charged with offence of "offering for sale" wild live birds

Judgement

- Appellant acquitted - advertisement was an invitation to treat.

- *Lord Parker CJ* - there was "business sense" in treating such advertisements as invitations to treat, seller could conclude contracts with many people, exposing him to contracts he could not perform.

- implied that the offer is only capable of acceptance "while stocks last"?

Cases where advertisement may be interpreted as offer rather than invitation to treat

Ex. Carlill v Carbolic Smoke Ball Co (1893)

Facts

- Manufacturers of the Carbolic Smoke ball, released an advert, in which they offered to give £100 to any person who caught flu by using their smoke balls.

- Claimant caught influenza after using the smoke ball in the specified manner

- She then claimed for the £100

Judgement

- Advertisement was an offer to the whole world

- Contract was made when the claimant performed the condition stated.

- Claimant entitled to recover £100

Auction Sales

- General rule is that an Auctioneer does not make an offer. He merely invites others to negotiate.

- Offers made by bids

- Offer is accepted when auctioneer strikes the table (British Car Auctions Ltd v Wright 1972)

- But "uncertainty" regarding the term "without reserve" - auction is to take place without a reserve price.

Ex. Warlow v Harrison (1959)

- Martin B stated obiter – here the auctioneer makes an offer that the sale will be without reserve and that that offer is accepted by the highest bidder at the auction.

- Offer is made by auctioneer and not owner of goods.

- This analysis affirmed by Court of Appeal

Ex. Barry v Davies (Trading as Heathcote Ball and Co) (2000)

- Collateral contract - contract that comes into existence between the auctioneer and the highest bidder
- Judge at first instance (Court of Appeal affirmed) - "there was a collateral contract between the auctioneer and the highest bidder constituted by an offer by the auctioneer to sell to the highest bidder which was accepted when the bid was made".

Issues with this analysis:

1. **At what point of time is the offer made by the auctioneer**

- Is it when advertisement of the auction without a reserve price is issued?
- Or is it when goods are actually put up for sale in the auction?
- No clear answer in authority.

1. **Should Barry should be employed in the case where an auction is held with a reserve price, and that price is exceeded during bidding**

- Once reserve price has been reached, the auctioneer cannot withdraw the lot from the sale, without incurring a liability for breach of a collateral contract to the highest bidder at the point in time at which the lot was withdrawn
- Barry and Warlow – possible example of court's reasoning backwards, decisions to give remedies for bidders.

Tenders

- Generally, the invitation to tender is an invitation treat.
- Offer then made by parties submitting a tender offer.
- Acceptance when issuer of tender accepts one of them.

However, in certain court cases, the court may hold that the invitation to tender was, in fact, an offer
Ex. Harvela Investments Ltd v Royal Trust Co of Canada (1986)
Facts

— First defendants sold their shares by sealed competitive tender

— Two parties submitted bids.

— Defendants stated that they would accept the highest offer received.

— Claimants tendered a bid of $2,175,000

— Second defendant tendered $2,100,000 or '$101,000' more than any other bid.

— First defendants accepted second defendants bid, treating it as a bid of $2,276,000

Judgement

— H of L - first defendants were bound to accept the claimants' bid

— Invitation to tender was an offer of a unilateral contract. They had committed to accept highest bid.

— The purpose of the tender was frustrated by the second defendant — the whole process was designed to find the highest price the parties were willing to pay. By just saying 'anything required' this could not occur fairly.

— What would happen if both parties submitted referential bids?

Ex. Blackpool and Fylde Aero Club Ltd v Blackpool BC (1990)
Flexible approach.
Facts

— Defendant local authority invited traders to operate pleasure flights from Blackpool airport.

— Tender stated that: "the council do not bind themselves to accept all or any part of the tender. No tender which is received after the last date and time specified shall be admitted for consideration. Tenders had to be received by the town clerk not later than 12'0'clock noon on Thursday 17 March'.

— Claimants posted bid at 11am on 17 March.

– Letter box was not emptied at 12'O'Clock noon, defendants did not receive before the deadline and so did not consider it.

– Claimants brought action for damages for, inter alia, breach of contract

– However, if invitation to tender is only an invitation to treat, no contract had been concluded, and no action could be maintained.

Judgement

– The defendants were contractually obliged to consider the tender

– For breach of that obligation, they were liable in damages.

Court adopted a *two-contract analysis*

1. Contract was concluded with the party whose tender was accepted

2. Invitation to tender also constituted a unilateral offer to "consider" any offer submitted. This offer was accepted, and so a contract occurred.

Complexities/Problems with the this:
When will a duty to consider occur? Council did not expressly accept an obligation to consider conforming tenders, but the court saw fit to imply such a duty
Court of appeal relied on a number of inconclusive factors

1. Invitation to tender to small number of parties

2. The intention of the parties

3. The tender procedure was "clear, orderly, and familiar". The more precise a statement is, the easier it will be to find it an offer.

Difficulty lies in determining the scope of this "duty to consider"

– Could defendants have rejected all tenders - appears so

– Stocker LJ - obligation to consider "would not preclude or in-hibit the council from deciding not to accept any tender or to award the concession, provided the decision was bonafide and honest, to any tenderer".

Time-tables and vending machines

Examples of difficulty in making a distinction between an offer and an invitation.
Ex. Wilkie v London Transport Board 1947
Different analysis – Getting on a bus

1. Lord Greene - offer made by bus company, and it is accepted when the 'passenger puts himself either on the platform or inside the bus'.

2. Acceptance takes place when the passenger asks for a ticket and pays the fare?

3. Bus timetable is an invitation to treat? Offer made when the passenger boards the bus, and acceptance takes place when bus conductor accepts the money and issues a ticket?

4. Bus conductor makes the offer when he issues the ticket, ac-cepted on payment?

Consequences if...
Ticket contains an exclusion clause; when would exclusion apply? Notice?
Ex. Thornton v Shoe Lane Parking Ltd (1971)

– Lord Denning – Automatic ticket machine outside a carpark made offers which were accepted by those who then drove into the car park.

Acceptance

– **Acceptance** – statement of assent to the terms of an offer.

– Carlill v Carbolic Smoke Ball Co 1893 – can accept by conduct.

– **Conduct** - only acceptance if offeree did the act with the in-tention, objectively assessed, of acceptance (Day Morris As-sociates v Voyce 2003)

- **Purported acceptance** – an 'acceptance' which introduces new terms cannot be acceptance; instead, it is a counteroffer.

- **Counter-offer** - "kills off" the original offer.

Ex. Hyde v Wrench 1840
Facts

- Defendant offered to sell some land for £1000.

- Claimant offered to purchase the land for £950

- Defendant refused £950

- Claimant wrote to defendant agreeing to pay £1000. This was refused.

Judgement

- There was no contract between the parties

- Claimant's offer of £950 was a counter-offer which killed off the defendant's original offer, could not now be accepted to form a contract.

Communication of the acceptance

- Acceptance must be communicated to the offeror

- Must be brought to the attention of the offeror.

Ex. Entores v Miles Far East Corp (1955)
Denning LJ

- If an oral acceptance cannot be heard due to overflying aircraft, then there is no contract unless the acceptor repeats his acceptance, once the noise has subsided.

- If line goes dead on phone, the acceptor must telephone the offeror to make sure that he has heard the acceptance

- Where acceptance is made clearly, it is for the offeror to let the offeree know they have not heard or understood.

Instantaneous communication - acceptance takes place at the moment the acceptance is received (Brinkibon Ltd v Stahag Stahl 1983)

Acceptance in ignorance of the offer

English law – if a person ignorant to an offer, performs the requested act, they cannot sue for breach of contract. *(Gibbons v Proctor 1891)*

- Importance is in clarity – not enough to find agreement and synchronised intention, need a clear offer and a clear acceptance.

- Similarly, in *Tinn v Hoffman & Co 1873*, cross-offers which are identical only create a contract when one offer is accepted.

- These points reinforce that contract law adopts an objective approach to agreement.

- Must have offer in mind when performing an 'acceptance' act. In *R v Clarke (1927)* - party claiming reward forgot about the offer at the time he gave the information, hence he was not entitled to the reward.

Prescribed method of acceptance

- Offeror is not bound unless the terms of his offer are complied with, including prescribed methods of acceptance.

- Must be clearly communicated

- Where the offeror has not been clear, court will allow acceptance which is made in a form which is no less advantageous to him than the form prescribed.

- In *Manchester Diocesan Council for Education v Commercial and General Investments Ltd (1969)* acceptance posted to the wrong address, but a relevant address and one which would allow for easy communication with the address in the tender was held to be valid.

Acceptance by silence

- Silence cannot constitute acceptance.

- Rationale - unfair to put an offeree in a position where they must do something to avoid the imposition of unwanted contractual arrangements

Ex. Felthouse v Bindley (1862)
Facts

- Claimant and nephew negotiated for sale of nephew's horse.

- Claimant stated that if he heard nothing further from his nephew, then he considered the horse his at the agreed price.

- Nephew did not respond to this offer but decided to accept it and told an auctioneer now not to sell it.

- Auctioneer mistakenly sold horse

Judgement

- Nephews silence did not amount to an acceptance of the offer

But.... In comparison to...
The Hannah Blumenthal

- H of L - contract to abandon reference to arbitration could be concluded by the silence of both parties

Cie Francaise d'Importation et de Distribution SA v Deutsche Continental Handelsgesellschaft (1985)

- Bingham J - "some violence... to familiar rules of contract such as the requirement that acceptance of an offer should be communicated to the offeror unless the requirement of communication is expressly or impliedly waived".

- However, no case sought to overrule/question explicitly the correctness of *Felthouse v Bindley*

- Reasoning in arbitration cases distorted, as neither arbitrators'/ courts had the power to dismiss an arbitration for want of prosecution

But arbitration cases also remind us that **silence does not amount to an acceptance, is not an absolute rule:**
Ex. Vitol SA v Norelf Ltd (1996)
Lord Steyn citing case of *Rust v Abbey Life Assurance Co Ltd (1979)* - "our law does in exceptional cases recognise acceptance of an offer by silence".

– General rule is intended to protect the offeree, and should not apply where its application would cause hardship to the offeree.

Exceptions to the rule requiring communication of acceptance

Rule that acceptance needs to be communicated is not absolute:

– Carlill c Carbolic Smoke Ball Co 1893 – example where terms do not insist upon acceptance.

– Offeror may be prevented by his conduct from arguing that the acceptance was communicated to him (Entores v Miles Far East Corp 1955)

...But most controversial exception occurs where acceptance sent through post

Postal acceptance

English law - acceptance takes place when the letter of acceptance is posted by the offeree (Adam v Lindsell 1818)

– Justifications

Justification: Post office is the agent of the offeror: receipt by agent = receipt by offeror.
Criticism: Agent link is weak, Post office has no power to contract for the offeror.
Justification: The offeror opted for postal negotiations; therefore they should be the party to assume the risks of postal dealings.
Criticism: This isn't necessarily true. Could be the case that the offeree initiated negotiations through the post, by asking the offeror for the terms on which he was prepared to do business
Validity of this Justification:
Henthorn v Fraser (1892) - postal rule only applies where it is reasonable to use the post
This doesn't necessarily mean the offeror should assume the risks.
Justification: Offeree should not be prejudiced once he has dispatched his acceptance, and he should be able to rely on the efficacy of his acceptance
Criticism: This argument is strong and protects the offeree, however, a counter argument can be made that the rule doesn't support the

offeror as they cannot revoke an offer as soon as acceptance is posted, they can be in a valid contract before they know it.

Why was the postal rule adopted?

Initial adoption may lie in the public perception of the postal service in the middle of the nineteenth century

1. Uniform Penny Post introduced 1837

2. Postage began to be pre-paid

– Gardener – this means that public perception at the time was that, a letter once posted, it would be delivered "without further subvention from outside the system", and that this led to the "notional equation of the posting of a letter with its delivery".

– This is not now relevant or realistic; we have instant communication via text, phone, email. Therefore, the idea that putting a letter in the post is not analogous to these forms of communication. No one now assumes posting is same as delivery.

– Byrne v Van Tienhoven (1880) – represents a narrowing of the rule.

– Rule can be seen as continuing to exist in a world which is completely different to the world in which the rule was established.

General rule gives rise to practical difficulties

1. **Letter of acceptance is lost in the post**

– Application of general rule leads to contract being concluded if sent initially (*Household Fire Insurance v Grant (1879)*.

– Rejected in Scotland, in *Mason v Benhar Coal Co 1882,* by Lord Shand

– Lord Shand - "no contract came into existence when the acceptance was posted, but never reached the offeror".

– But, English law is still committed to postal acceptance rule, even when lost.

– Korbetis v Transgrain Shipping BV (2005) – if addressed wrongly by offeree, acceptance does not occur.

1. **Offeree posts his acceptance and sends a rejection by a quicker method so that the rejection reaches the offeror before the acceptance**

– General rule- contract already concluded when rejection is sent.

– This does though create an absurd circumstance where both parties rely on the fact that a contract has not been concluded, when in fact the earlier acceptance had concluded a contract.

– But it can be argued, that it would be absurd to hold that a contract had been concluded when both parties relied on the fact that there was no contract (although in this case it can be said that both parties entered into a second contract under which they agreed to abandon their rights and obligations under the first contract)

– However, if rejection is valid, offeree could hedge their bets by sending an acceptance and waiting to see if the bargain was a good one. If the bargain was bad, they could, therefore, exploit the rule by sending a rejection in a faster manner than their acceptance. This would provide the offeree with more power than the offeror.

– Unclear as to which of these approaches adopted in English law.

Practical difficulties results in the postal rule being subject to limitations

1. Must be reasonable for the offeree to use the post.

2. Can contract out of rule by only accepting when post reaches.

3. Rule not used in many cases where the parties have not been dealing face-to-face.

– *Ex. Entores v Miles Far East Corp* - held that postal rule confined to non-instantaneous forms of communication

– Distinction in forms of communication – only posted acceptances under the rule.

– Email not covered by the postal rule (Thomas v BPE Solicitors 2010)

1. *Holwell Solicitors Ltd v Hughes (1974) rule:* won't apply - "where it would lead to manifest inconvenience and absurdity". Very wide.

Alternative:

– Abolish the general rule, replace it with the rule that acceptance takes place when acceptance is received by the offeror,

– With only qualification being that the offeror cannot revoke the offer once the acceptance has been posted (**Articles 16 (1)/18 (2) United Nations Convention on Contracts for the International Sale of Goods (Vienna Convention) and Articles 2:202 (1)/2:205 (1) of the Principles of European Contract Law)**

Acceptance in unilateral contracts

– **Unilateral contract** – contract where a party is offered something in return for performing a prescribed act. (Carlill v Carbolic Smoke Ball Co 1893)

– *Effect of classifying contract unilateral and not bilateral* - acceptance can be made by fully performing the requested act; without needing to give a statement as to this intention or conduct.

Difficulties regarding unilateral contracts

Difficulty in determining the point at which an offer has been accepted. This is vitally important in determining when an offer can be withdrawn.

Does full performance constitute acceptance, does half performance?

English Law - "true view of a unilateral contract must, in general, be that the offeror is entitled to require full performance of the condition which he has imposed and short of that he is not bound, that must be subject to one important qualification, which stems from the fact that there must be an implied obligation on the part of the of-

feror not to prevent the condition becoming satisfied, which obligation it seems to me must arise as soon as the offeree starts to perform" *(Goff LJ - Daulia Ltd v Four Millbank Nominees Ltd 1978)*
How far is court willing to imply an obligation not to prevent the condition becoming satisfied?

Two cases:

Ex. Errington v Errington (1952)

Facts

- Father purchased a house for £750, using a mortgage for £500

- His son and Daughter-in-law moved into the house. The father made a statement that the couple could have the house if they took care of the mortgage.

- Couple began repayments.

- Father died, and his representatives attempted to cancel the arrangement.

Judgement

- Court of Appeal - the father's promise was a unilateral contract".

- Couple had embarked upon performance, and this meant the representatives could not revoke the deal.

- Only case where they could would be if they left performance "incomplete and unperformed" (Soulsebury v Soulsebury 2008).

However

Ex. Luxor (Eastbourne) Ltd v Cooper (1941)

Facts

- Claimant agreed with defendant's that he would receive commission for introducing buyers for their cinemas.

- Claimants succeeded and found buyers, however, the defendants did not complete the deal.

Judgement

- Claimant was not entitled to the commission.

- The commission was only payable when the sale was completed.

- H of L - there was a common understanding the commission was related to the sale. The claimant has taken "the risk in the hope of a substantial remuneration for a comparatively small exertion".

Termination of the offer

Five ways an offer may be terminated:

1. **Withdrawn**

- Offer can be withdrawn by the offeror if it has not been accepted.

- Notice of withdrawal must be brought to offeree. Just needs to be communicated to the offeree, not by the offeror.

Ex. Dickinson v Dodds (1876) –
A Defendant withdrew his offer to sell a house, and this was communicated to the offeree who then tried to submit an acceptance. This was not held to form a contract.
Rule that withdrawal must brought to the attention of the offeree has odd effects, with regards to offers sent through post
Ex. Byrne v Tienhoven (1880)

- For the purpose of withdrawing an offer, the postal rule does not apply.

- In this case, an offer was send and immediately accepted by post, following this (and before the acceptance arrived) the offeror sent a withdrawal.

- Contract was concluded.

- Objective determination of agreement.

Not entirely clear when the revocation is treated as being brought to his attention

– No clear English authority on this point (when reads it or when the letter reaches his business).

The Brimnes (1975)

– Court of Appeal - notice of withdrawal of a vessel sent by telex in ordinary business hours, withdrawal became effective when it was received in this context.

– No requirement that it be read.

1. **Offer terminated by a rejection by the offeree**

– Rejection or counter-offer kills the original offer (Hyde v Wrench)

1. **Offer may be terminated by lapse of time**

– Can set a specific time period, beyond which acceptance is not valid.

– Offer without time limit is open for a reasonable time period.

1. **Offer which is conditional on ending if a specific event occurs, will not be open to acceptance if that event happens.**

2. **Offer may be terminated by the death of the offeror**

– Law not entirely clear on this point, death may terminate offers because the parties cannot enter into an agreement once one of the parties is dead.

– Offeree cannot accept an offer once he knows that the offeror has died. For contracts of personal services, even an acceptance in ignorance of an offeror's death cannot be valid.

– No authority on the position where it is the offeree who dies

The limits of offer and acceptance
There are many difficulties with regards to the offer and acceptance model

– many modern transactions simply do not fit the simple offer/acceptance model.

– offer and acceptance is based on a relatively simple concept – the mirror principle, requiring an offer and a matching acceptance. Yet grey areas can be shown in common transactions such as shopping purchases, buying a bus ticket or even accepting an offer through the post.

– **For each of these issues, there is a balancing act between upholding, respecting and actioning the intention of parties and managing the interests of justice.**

– Like any rule in contract, the need for clarity represents another challenge.

A more certain solution?
Ex. Article 19 of the Vienna Convention on Contracts for the International Sale of Goods

(1) A reply to an offer which purports to be an acceptance but contains additions, limitations or other modifications is a rejection of the offer and constitutes a counter-offer

(2) However, a reply to an offer which purports to be an acceptance but contains additional or different terms which do not materially alter the terms of the offer constitutes an acceptance, unless the offeror, without undue delay, objects orally to the discrepancy or dispatches a notice to that effect. If he does not so object, the terms of the contract are the terms of the offer with the modifications contained in the acceptance

(3) Additional or different terms relating, among other things, to the price, payment, quality, and quantity of the goods, place of delivery, extent of one party's liability to the other or the settlement of disputes are considered to alter the terms of the offer materially

– This approach attempts to provide a clear, certain rule while maintaining a degree of agility to counter difficult cases.

Is Article 19 itself too uncertain?

1. Does any alteration suggested by the offeror count as a "addition, limitation or other modification" or is some minimum standard required?

2. How far does the definition of 'materially' in p3 stretch?

— None of the legislative solutions proposed for battle of the forms cases has escaped criticism (McKendrick 1988).

— No single formula will work for every case.

— With infinitely variable intentions of parties, the possibility of finding absolute certainty in a rule is severely restricted.

— Ultimately, Article 19 too rigid.

— Present law is a reasonable means of balancing the competing interests of certainty, justice, and respect for the intentions of parties.

— Flexible application of model by the courts is crucial to this.

2. Intention to Create Legal Relations

Summary

- An agreement with consideration does not necessarily create a legally enforceable contract.

- A further element of 'Intention to create legal relations' is also needed for all contracts.

- Different arguments as to the basis of the doctrine – both concern for the facilitating intention of parties and public policy reasons come into play.

- The public policy argument can be shown here, "it is, generally, right that courts should not enforce entirely social engagements, such as arrangements to play squash or come to dinner, even though the parties themselves may intend to be legally bound thereby" - *Scottish Law Commission (1977)*.

- The doctrine, in practice, relies on a distinction between domestic and commercial agreements.

Balfour v Balfour (1919)

- Wife was promised £30 per month by her husband, while he worked abroad.

- Wife tried to enforce this promise.

- This failed for two reasons: the wife did not provide consideration, and both parties did not intend their agreement to be legally enforceable.

- **Atkin LJ** - "agreements such as these are outside the realm of contracts altogether. The common law does not regulate the form of agreements between spouses... The consideration that really obtains for them is that neutral love and affection which counts for so little in these cold Courts".
Reasoning:

- **Atkin LJ** decision to exclude this form of agreement from contract appears to be based on public policy, "it would be of the worst possible example to hold that agreements such as this resulted in legal obligations which could be enforced in the courts... the small courts of this country would have to be multiplied one hundredfold if these arrangements were held to result in legal obligations"

- Decision clearly rooted in policy and a desire to avoid unnecessary litigation. Ruling appears to cast doubt over importance of parties intentions for this test.

- Ruling has been interpreted as a presumption that parties to domestic and social agreements do not intend to create legal relations.

- Intention to create legal relations divided in **two categories**

- **Domestic and social agreements -** presumption is that no legal relations were intended.

- **Commercial agreements -** presumption is that parties did intend to create legal relations

- Initial presumption may be rebutted by evidence of contrary intention. This is difficult given the strength of the presumptions.

- **Hedley (1985)** - "keeping contract in its place, to keep it in the commercial sphere and out of domestic cases, except when judges think it has a useful role to play"

Rebutting the presumption

- Evidence of intention is relevant to rebuttal of presumption.

- The importance of intention is limited for two reasons.

1. In domestic and social agreements parties may not have a clear intention

2. The strength of the initial presumption.

- Commercial agreements - presumption of legal relations (heavy one), which isn't discharged easily (Edwards v Skyways [1964] 1 WLR 349.

- Marginal role of intention demonstrated by examining scope of two presumptions and then factors which are relevant to the rebuttal of these presumptions

Domestic and Social agreements

Agreements between husband and wife and agreements between parents and children are presumed not to be legally binding.

Jones v Padavatton (1969)

- Mother persuaded daughter to read for the English Bar and promised to pay her $200 maintenance per month.

- Mother bought a house in London for daughter; she would live rent free and use the proceeds of letting the other rooms for her maintenance.

- Daughter then fell out with her mother.

- Mother then sought possession of house with the daughter relying on her agreement as a defence.

- Court of Appeal - agreement was not held to be legally binding, and mother was entitled to possession

Factors which determine whether presumption has been rebutted:

In order to rebut the presumptions, mere subjective intention is not sufficient. The court must be able to find evidence of an objective intention.

1. Context - if courts perceive that a family agreement has been entered, which is reminiscent of a "business context", court will find the presumption has been rebutted.

- *Ex. Granatino v Radmacher (2010)* - presumption rebutted when husband and wife enter into an "Agreement to share the ownership or tenancy of the matrimonial home, bank accounts, savings or other assets".

– *Ex. Merritt v Merritt (1970) and Soulsbury v Soulsbury (2007)* - in divorce situations or separations, presumptions do no operate because parties "bargain keenly" and rely on "honourable understandings".

1. Reliance - if one party acts to his detriment on the faith of the agreement, court would be more willing to determine that agreement intended to create legal relations.

Ex. Parker v Clark (1960) –

– Defendants (elderly people) suggested that claimants (friends) to come live with them. Claimants agreed but stated that they would sell their house.

– Defendants stated that this problem could be resolved by claimants leaving a share of their house to them in their will.

– Both parties fell out, and the defendants asked the claimants to move out. Claimants left and brought action against defendants for breach of contract. Defendants stated there was no intention to create legal relations.

– *Devlin J* - held that parties did intend to create legal relations. "I cannot believe that the defendant thought that the law would leave him at liberty...if he chose to tell the claimants that he had changed his mind, that they could take their furniture away, and that he was indifferent whether they found anywhere else to live or not".

1. Certainty - court consider certainty of agreement entered into by parties
   Ex. Vaughan v Vaughan (1953)

– A husband promised his deserted wife she could stay in the matrimonial home.

– It was held this promise was too vague and therefore could not create contractual relations.

– The court relied on the evidence that the terms of the promise were not discussed or agreed.

Commercial agreements

Strong presumptions that parties do intend to create legal relations. *Ex. Esso Petroleum Ltd v Comrs of Customs and Excise (1976)* –

- Esso supplied garages with world cup coins 1970,

- Garages were told to give away one coin for every 4 gallons of petrol they sold.

- The coins were subjected to purchase tax on grounds that they had been sold.

- However, it was held that coins were not supplied under a contract of sale.

- *H of L divided on issue of intention to create legal relations:*

- The majority found there was intention. *Lord Simon, Lord Wilberforce, and Lord Fraser* argued there was a bargain of some sort between garage and customer.

- However, *Lord Russell and Viscount Dilhorne* argued because the coins were "going free" there was no intention to create legal relations.

- Express terms of a contract can rebut the presumptions.

- This intention must though be made clearly and explicitly.

- For example, an agreement made "subject to contract", cannot create legal relations.

3. What is a Term?

What is a term?

A contract is made up of different terms, agreed by the parties. Not everything said by the parties while negotiating a contract is terms of that contact – what is actually said can be categorised in one of three ways:

- **Mere opinion** – these statements have no legal effect, they are loose and casual.

- **Term** – failure to comply with a term is a breach of contract.

- **Mere representation** – failure to comply does not lead to a breach; the innocent party must instead claim damages for misrepresentation or have the contract set aside.

Intention is key; the question is why the statement was made. *Courts use an objective test, together with some established principles.*

Judicial principles:

Verification

A statement cannot be a term of contract if the party making it asks another party to verify its truth.

- *Ecay v Godfrey (1947)* - Seller of boat said boat was of good quality but recommended it should be surveyed (mere representation).

If the maker of a statement explicitly discourages verification, the opposite result is found.

- *Schawel v Reade (1913)* – Owner of horse said it was sound, and advised against checking this. Claimant relied, statement held to be a term.

Importance

If a statement is so important that the party would not have entered into the contract but for it, it is likely to be treated as a term.

- *Couchman v Hill (1947)* - Claimant informed by defendant that heifer was not in calf. Claimant stated that he would not purchase it if this was not true. Seven weeks after the purchase, heifer had a miscarriage and died. Statement held to be a term due to its importance.

Special Knowledge

If the party making a statement has special knowledge or skill in comparison with the receiver of the statement, the statement may be held to be a term. Similarly, where knowledge is equal statements may be held to be mere representations.

- *Oscar Chess Ltd v Williams (1957)* - Defendants sold car to claimants for £290, which was, in fact, worth far less owing to it being a much older model than parties thought. Log book detailing car as a newer model was discovered to be a forgery. Defendant was in good faith. Claimants, who were car dealers, were in a position to actually know the true age of the car hence the statement of its age was held to be a mere representation.

- *Dick Bentley Productions Ltd v Harold Smith (Motors) Ltd (1965)* – Claimant asked defendants (car dealers) to find a suitable car. Claimants found a car and stated it had done a certain number of miles, in fact, their statement was grossly under the real mileage. Due to their knowledge, the defendants' statement was held to be a term.

The consequences of the distinction between a term and a mere representation

- *Misrepresentation Act 1967* - damages available for misrepresentation in a wide range of circumstances

- The amount of damages recoverable, is the question now, rather than whether damages are recoverable at all.

In the case of a statement being:

- **Term** - breach of term would entitle innocent party to recover damages, putting them in the position that they would have been in, had the contract been performed. This is known as the expectation interest.

- **Mere representation** - damages only available to compensate representee for losses made through reliance on misrepresentation

The ability to set aside a contract is also affected by the term/representation distinction.

- For representations, a representee can always set aside a contract.

- For terms, an innocent party can only set aside the contract if the term broken is a condition, not a warranty.

Can a representation be incorporated into a contract as a term?

Pennsylvania Shipping Co v Comagnie Nationale de Navigation (1936) -
Claimants chartered a tanker from defendants. During negotiations, the defendants gave statements which were false about the heating of the ship. This false information then became included in the contract. When the claimants found out about the incorrect nature of the information, they attempted to have the contract set aside for misrepresentation.

Branson J - representation "merged in the higher contractual right", and on the grounds of misrepresentation, there was no need to set aside the contract. Claimants were actually claiming for breach of contract.

Misrepresentation Act 1967 - representee who's entered into a contract after misrepresentation, may rescind the contract for misrepresentation, even though misrepresentation is incorporated into the contract, provided that he would otherwise be entitled to rescind the contract .

4. The Sources of Contractual Terms

Contractual terms

Express terms - terms agreed orally or in writing by parties.
Orally – question of fact. Can be tricky.
Writing (difficulties that arise) -

- Can courts go outside the written agreement to find additional terms to the contract

- The effect of signature

- How written terms can be included in a contract – by notice, by standard dealings.

Implied terms - terms which are implied into the contract by the courts or by Parliament – these are not specifically agreed in writing or orally by the parties to a contract.

The parol evidence rule

- **"Parol evidence rule"** – when contracting parties choose to use a written document, the parties cannot make use of extrinsic evidence to add to, vary or contradict that document; the document is the sole record of terms of the contract *(Jacobs v Batavia & General Plantations Trust Ltd 1924)*

Purpose of the rule

Certainty.
Ex. Shogun Finance Ltd v Hudson (2003)

- *Lord Hobhouse* - "The parol evidence rule is fundamental to the mercantile law of this country and that the certainty of the contract depends on it. The rule is one of the great strengths of English commercial law and is one of the main reasons for the international success of English law in preference to laxer systems which do not provide the same certainty".

31

Problems with the rule

- Rigid application can lead to injustice.

- Ex. If written document is procured by fraud, innocent party would wish to lead extrinsic evidence to demonstrate the fraud.

- *Exceptions* therefore important.

Exceptions

1. **Rule does not apply where the written document was not intended to contain the whole of the agreement (Allen v Pink 1838)**

- *Wedderburn (1959)* - reduces the rules to "no more than a self-evident tautology... when the writing is the whole contract, the parties are bound by it, and parol evidence is excluded; when it is not, evidence of the other terms must be admitted".

- Law Commission (1986) – rule is "no more than a circular statement".

- Based on this, rule does not create injustice, will not prevent a party from leading evidence of terms which were intended to be part of the contract

- However, courts will assume document that appears to be contract, is the whole contract.

- Presumption is rebuttable; this means it is highly unlikely that the parol evidence rule will stop a party from leading evidence of terms which were intended to be part of the contract

Parol evidence is admissible....

1. To demonstrate terms which must be implied into the agreement (Gillespie Bros & Co v Cheney, Eggar &Co 1896)

2. To show a custom which must be implied into the contract (Hutton v Warren 1836)

3. To prove invalidity on the grounds of misrepresentation, mistake, fraud, or non-est factum (Campbell Discount Co v Gall 1961)

4. To demonstrate the document should be rectified

5. To prove the contract has not yet come into operation or that it has stopped operating (Pym v Campbell 1856)

6. To demonstrate a collateral agreement exists (Mann v Nunn 1874)

Ex. City and Westminster Properties (1934) Ltd v Mudd (1959)
Facts

— Lease agreement between parties contained a covenant stating the tenant could use the premises just for business.

— Tenant signed lease after oral assurance by the lessors' agent, that the lessors would not object to using the premises as residence.

— Action by lessors to forfeit the lease because tenant was using for residence.

Judgement

— Evidence of the assurance given by the lessors' agent was admissible. This was despite clear contradiction with express terms.

Criticism

— Seems to contradict Angell v Duke (1875) and Henderson v Arthur (1907)

— However, if collateral agreement is a separate argument, no clear justification as to why this should have to be consistent with written agreement.

— Undermining of parol evidence rule

— Width of the exceptions may actually undermine the initial purpose of ensuring certainty.

— Can be doubted whether the rule exists in English law.

— Law Commission recommended in a working paper (1976) - that the parol evidence rule be abolished

In a recent paper (1986) - *concluded that no legislative action need to be taken for 2 reasons:*

1. Rule didn't stop courts from using extrinsic evidence where this was consistent with the parties' intentions.

2. Legislative change would now lead to more confusion.

   – Hence rule remains.

   – However, given width of the exceptions, unlikely to have significant effect in practice.

Bound by your signature?

   – Rule - *person is bound by a document which he signs, even if they do not read it.*

Ex. L'Estrange v F Graucob Ltd (1934)

Facts

   – Claimant was sold an automatic slot machine by the defendants

   – She signed a form that contained a clause excluding liability for all warranties

   – When machine did not work, claimant brought an action against the defendants for breach of an implied warranty – warranty being that product would be fit for purpose.

Judgement

   – Defendants had excluded their liability. The clause doing this was incorporated into the contract by the claimant's signature

   – Small print didn't mean anything.

   – Seems harsh for the customer.

But...
Ex. Grogan v Robin Meredith Plant Hire (1996)
Facts

– Document signed by defendants was a time sheet for the hire of machinery which stated, "All hire undertaken under CPA conditions. Copies available on request" (bottom of page)

Judgement

– Indemnity clause contained under CPA conditions was not incorporated by signature.

– Auld LJ - "too mechanistic" to say signature incorporates everything referenced on a sheet.

Courts must consider whether document signed, should be regarded as...

– **Contractual document** - giving it contractual effect

– **Administrative document** - designed to enable parties to give effect to their prior agreement

Final judgement in Grogan v Robin Meredith Plant Hire (1996)

– Timesheet not found to have contractual effect

– Courts focussed on the nature of the document.

What if document **is intended to have contractual effect**, and party trying to enforce it knows the other party to the agreement has neither read or understood the terms within?
Ex. Tilden Rent-a-car Co v Clendenning (1978) (Ontario Court)

– Signature could only be relied upon as evidence of genuine consent.

Signs of a resurgence in judicial support for the rule in L'Estrange

Ex. Toll (FGCT) Pty Ltd v Alphapharm Pty Ltd (2004) (Australian High Court)

– Challenge to the rule rejected in robust terms

Ex. Peekay Intermark Ltd v Australia and NZ Banking Group Ltd (2006)

— Moore-Bick LJ - "the rule in L'Estrange is an important principle of English law, which underpins the whole of commercial life; any erosion of it would have serious repercussions".

Parliaments role

— **The Unfair Contract Terms Act 1977** - controls on exclusion clauses, like the type found in L'Estrange

— **The Unfair Terms in Consumer Contracts Regulations 1999** - consumer context- small print.

— *1(i) of Schedule 2 to the Regulations* - "a term which has the object or effect of irrevocably binding the consumer to terms with which he had no real opportunity of becoming acquainted before the conclusion of the contract, is indicatively unfair".

— This provision attacks the L'Estrange rule by regulating the term which seeks to incorporate the onerous terms into the contract — rather than looking at the implication of a signature.

— *1(b) of Schedule 2 to the Regulations* - "inappropriately excluding or limiting the legal rights of the consumer vis-a-vis the seller or supplier... in the event of total or partial non-performance or inadequate performance by the seller or supplier of any of the contractual obligations".

— L'Estrange rule will not apply if the signature has been produced by fraud/misrepresentation, or where the defence of **non est factum** is made out:

Non est factum

— Illiterate person signed a deed which was incorrectly read to him by someone else.

— Illiterate person not bound by the deed. They could argue *non est factum* (this is not my deed)

Effect of non est factum - to render the deed void.

Problems with the doctrine

Competing policies:

1. The injustice of holding a person to a bargain entered without a consenting mind.

2. The desire to hold a person to a signed document, especially where innocent third parties rely to their detriment upon the validity of the signature

These competing policies are seen in the following cases:
Ex. Saunders v Anglia Building Society (1971)
Facts

- A widow of 78 made a will, leaving her house to a nephew

- The nephew wanted to raise money immediately on the security of the home

- Widow agreed, provided that she could live in her home for the rest of her life rent free

- Nephew did not want to raise the loan in his own name.

- Arrangement with a friend to raise the money on the security of the house

- Widow did not read the document because her glasses were broken, but she signed it after the friend assured her that it was a deed of gift to the nephew

- The friend raised money on a mortgage with the respondent building society but did not pay the nephew or the widow.

- Building society sought to recover possession of the property from the widow. Plead non est factum.

Judgement
In this case, there is the clash of the two competing policies

- H of L - gave greater weight to the policy of protecting an innocent party who had relied on signature and agreement, holding the defence of *non est factum* was not made out on the facts of the case

- Scott LJ (*Norwich and Peterborough Building Society v Steed 1993*) - the law in the main protects the innocent third party because "the signer of the document has, by signing, enabled the fraud to be carried out, enabled the false documents to go into circulation".

— *non est factum* is kept within very narrow confines

Scope of non est factum determined by 3 questions
1. **To whom is the plea available?**

— Originally only for those who were unable to read

— In *Saunders*, it was held that there was no confinement to those who are blind or illiterate

— Extends to those *"who are permanently or temporarily unable through no fault of their own to have without explanation any real understanding or purport of a particular document, whether that be from defective education, illness or innate incapacity"*

1. **For what type of mistake is the defence available?**

— Originally had to go to heart of the transaction *(Foster v Mackinnon 1869)*

— *Howatson v Webb (1907)* - Warrington J found a distinction between a mistake as to the "character" of the document and a mistake as to its "content"; the former being sufficient to support the plea of *non est factum*

— H of L rejected this distinction in *Saunders* — deemed "Arbitrary".

— Held difference must be radical, substantial, or fundamental

1. **When is a person prevented from relying on the defence?**

— If there is some carelessness from the person who signs the document.

Ex. United Dominions Trust Ltd v Western (1976)
Facts

— Defendant signed a loan agreement with the claimant company related to car purchase.

— Let garage owner complete details, including the price

— Garage owner increased the price of the car. Paid in good faith.

Judgement

— Onus on the defendant to prove he had acted carefully

— Held that the defendant had wholly failed to discharge that onus and therefore could not invoke the defence of *non est factum*

— If defence of non est factum cannot be proved...

— May be a remedy in misrepresentation, fraud or undue influence (Avon Finance Co v Bridger 1985)

— But misrepresentation, fraud or undue influence only render the contract voidable, and so greater protection is thereby afforded to 3rd party rights

Incorporation of written terms

— Contracting parties can agree to incorporate a set of written terms into their contract

Three obstacles to overcome before such terms can be incorporated:

1. **Notice of the terms must be given at or before the time of concluding the contract**

— Must be able to determine the precise moment when contract is concluded

Ex. Olley v Marlborough Court Ltd (1949)

— Notice in the bedroom of a hotel could not have been incorporated into a contract with a guest, because the notice was only seen by the guest after the contract had been concluded at the hotel reception desk

1. **Terms must be contained or referred to in a document which was intended to have contractual effect**

— Question of fact

Ex. Chapleton v Barry UDC (1940)
Facts

- Claimant hired a deck chair from the defendants

- On paying his money, he was given a ticket containing an exclusion clause – he was unaware of this at the time.

- Claimant was injured when he sat on chair which buckled.

- Defendants relied, by way of defence, on the exclusion clause contained in the ticket

Judgement

- Could not be relied on, because it was contained in a mere receipt which was not intended to have contractual effect

1. **Reasonable steps must be taken to bring the terms to the attention of the other party**

Ex. Parker v South Eastern Railway (1877)

- Not about whether the claimant read the notice.

Ex. Thompson v London, Midland and Scottish Railway Co Ltd (1930)

- Exclusion clause contained in a railway timetable was held to be validly incorporated, even if claimant could not read it.

- Result may be different if the party seeking to rely on the exclusion clause, knows of the disability of the other party (Richardson, Spence and Co Ltd v Rowntree 1894)

What amounts to a reasonable notice is a question which depends upon the facts and circumstances of the individual case?

- *Thompson* - held that the defendants took reasonable steps to bring the exclusion clause to the attention of the claimant, even though contained on page 552 of the timetable and timetable cost one-fifth of the price of the railway ticket.

- Today, if the clause is not referred to on the front of the ticket (Henderson v Stevenson 1875), and if the reference to the clause is obliterated (Sugar v London, Midland and Scottish Railway Co 1941), the clause is less likely to be incorporated into the contract

- *Ex. J Spurling Ltd v Bradshaw (1956)* - Denning LJ - "some clauses would need to be printed in red ink on the face of the document with a red hand pointing to it before the notice could be held to be sufficient" (red hand rule).

Interfoto Picture Library Ltd v Stiletto Visual Programmes Ltd (1989)
Facts

- Defendants ordered photographic transparencies from the claimants; they had not previously worked together.

- Claimants sent them 47 transparencies, together with a delivery note including some conditions.

- Condition 2 - holding fee of £5 per day was payable for every day the transparencies were kept more than 14 days

- Defendants for about the transparencies.

- They returned them after one month

- Claimants sent defendants an invoice for £3783.50.

Judgement

- Court of Appeal held that condition 2 was not incorporated into the contract, not enough notice.

- Party must prove that the term has been fairly and reasonably drawn to the attention of the other party, especially when particularly onerous or unusual.

- Bingham LJ - cases concerned with the question "whether it would in all the circumstances be fair to hold a party bound by any conditions... of an unusual and stringent nature".

The utility and application of this general principle is debateable

- Surely the defendants could have read the conditions on the delivery note (business context)

- Argument that condition 2 was a penalty clause (Bingham LJ)

Practical difficulties given rise to due to the use of a special test for the incorporation of onerous or unusual terms

- Practical difficulties – which terms meet this level.

- Words "onerous or unusual" are not "terms of art" (O'Brien v MGN Ltd [2002], Hale LJ) and courts have not been able to agree whether a particular term is or is not "onerous or unusual".

Ex. AEG (UK) Ltd v Logic Resource Ltd (1996)(Court of Appeal)

- Majority - clause requiring the purchaser to return the defective goods at his own expense not brought to attention in a fair and reasonable manner.

- Hobhouse LJ - "it is to be the policy of English law that in every case those clauses are to be gone through with, in effect, a toothcomb to see whether they were entirely unusual and entirely desirable in the particular contract, then one is completely distorting the contractual relationship between the parties and the ordinary mechanisms of making contracts. It will introduce uncertainty into the law of contract".

- Clause was subject to scrutiny under the Unfair Contract Terms Act 1977, and Hobhouse LJ view, "it was under the provisions of that act that problems of unreasonable clauses should be addressed, and the solution be found".

- More uncertainty.

but..

- Courts continue to apply a special rule to the incorporation of "onerous or unusual" terms in consumer and commercial transactions, due to difficulties in deciding which terms fall within the scope of the rule (Kaye v Nu Skin UK Ltd [2009])

Incorporation by a course of dealing

– Terms can be incorporated in a contract by a course of dealing

Ex. McCutcheon v David MacBrayne Ltd (1964)

– Course of dealing needs to be regular and consistent

– Depends upon the facts of the case

Ex. Henry Kendall Ltd v William Lillico ltd (1969)

– H of L - 100 similar contracts over 3 years constituted a course of dealing

Ex. Hollier v Rambler Motors (AMC) Ltd (1972)

– But in this case, three or four contracts over a period of five years was not.

– Equal bargaining power a consideration:

Ex. British Crane Hire Corp Ltd v Ipswich Plant Hire Ltd (1975)

– A clause incorporated after two previous transactions and a custom of the trade

– Court emphasised the fact that the parties were of equal bargaining power.

Course of dealing must not only be regular but also consistent
Ex. McCutcheon v David MacBrayne Ltd (1964)
Facts

– Ferry belonging to the defendants sank and the claimant's car lost

– Defendants tried to rely on an exclusion clause contained in a risk note; this was contrary to their usual practise, they had not asked the claimant's brother-in-law to sign.

Judgement

– H of L - No consistent course of dealing.

- Lord Pearce - there was no consistent course of dealing – always agreed in writing before – this was oral.

- This takes the requirement of consistency too far because only reason defendants relied on the course of dealing argument was that they had forgotten to ensure that the risk note was signed

- Knowledge of conditions inferred through the regularity and consistency of the course of dealing

- *McCutcheon* - Lord Devlin said previous dealings were only relevant if they demonstrated actual knowledge of the terms.

- Rejected by the H of L in *Henry Kendall Ltd v William Lillico Ltd*

Interpretation

- Contractual disputes arise because of disagreements about the proper interpretation

- Precedents are of limited value, because, "a decision on a different clause in a different context is seldom of much help on a question of construction" (Surrey Heath BC v Lovell Construction Ltd 1990)

- Some broad principles

- Courts, not the parties, decide what is the proper interpretation of the contract

- The court must seek to give effect to the intention of the parties

- This can at times be artificial.

- Illustration of this is the interpretation of exclusion clauses by the courts.

- Lord Diplock - "the reports are full of cases in which what would appear to be very strained constructions have been placed upon exclusion clauses" *(Photo Production Ltd v Securicor Transport Ltd 1980)*

Ways in which the court seeks to ascertain the intention of the parties

- Objective assessment of the wording of the contract and its surrounding circumstances

- Common law - "not to probe the real intentions of the parties but to ascertain the contextual meaning of the relevant contractual language. Intention is determined by reference to expressed rather than actual intention" *(Deutsche Genossenschaftsbank v Burnhope 1995)*

- Intention must be ascertained from the document that parties have elected to use to enshrine their agreement (Lovell & Christmas Ltd v Wall 1911)

Ex. Lovell & Christmas Ltd v Wall (1911)

- literal approach

- Cozens Hardy MR - "it is the duty of the court... to construe the document according to the ordinary grammatical meaning of the words used therein."

- shift in the literal approach, towards a purposive approach to interpretation;

Lord Steyn *(Deutsche Genossenschaftsbank v Burnhope 1995):*

- "parallel to the shift during the last two decades from a literalist to a purposive approach to the construction of statutes there has been a movement from a strict or literal method of construction of commercial contracts towards an approach favouring a commercially sensible construction".

Lord Steyn (Lord Napier and Ettrick v RF Kershaw Ltd 1999):

- "Loyalty to the text of a commercial contract, instrument, or document read in its contextual setting is the paramount principle of interpretation. But in the process of interpreting the meaning of the language of a commercial document the court ought generally to favour a commercially sensible construction. The reason for this approach is that a commercial construction is likely to give effect to the intention of the parties. Words ought therefore to be interpreted in the way in which a reasonable commercial person would construe them. And the reasonable commercial person can safely be assumed to be unimpressed with technical interpretations and undue emphasis on niceties of language".

Lord Hoffman (Investors Compensation Scheme Ltd v West Bromwich Building Society 1998)

— Lord Hoffman: the result of the new principles is to "assimilate the way in which such documents are interpreted by judges to the common sense principles by which any serious utterance would be interpreted in ordinary life.... almost all the old intellectual baggage of legal interpretation has been discarded".

Five principles

1. Interpretation must be the ascertainment of the meaning which the document would demonstrate to a reasonable person with all the background knowledge which would reasonably have been available to the parties at the time of contracting.

2. The background...[is] the "matrix of the fact". Must have been reasonably available to the parties.

3. The law excludes from the admissible background any previous negotiations of the parties and their declarations of subjective intent. They are admissible only in an action for rectification.

4. The meaning which a document (or any other utterance) would convey to a reasonable man is not the same thing as the meaning of its word.

5. The "rule" that words should be given their "natural and ordinary meaning" reflects the common sense proposition that we do not easily accept that people have made linguistic mistakes, particularly in formal documents.

— Shift shown in Mannai Investment Co Ltd v Eagle Star Life Assurance Co Ltd [1997]) and (Total Gas Marketing Ltd v Arco British Ltd [1998])

– Where language used by parties is unambiguous, it is the duty of the court to apply that meaning, even if the result is thought to be improbable (Rainy Sky SA v Kookmin Bank [2011])

Four principal issues that merit this discussion

1. **The shift towards a purposive approach generates too much uncertainty**

– How will courts find commercial purpose of the transaction?

– When will they chose to depart from ordinary meanings?

– What evidence will be needed before taking the step of rejecting the dictionary meaning?

– Claim that modern approach has produced too much uncertainty is indicative of the House of Lord finding it very difficult to reach agreement on issues of interpretation

Case: Mannai Investment Co Ltd v Eagle Star Life Assurance Co Ltd
House Divided: 3:1
Case: Deutsche Genossenschaftsbank v Burnhope
House Divided: 4:1
Case: Bank of Credit and Commerce International SA v Ali
House Divided: 4:1

Dissents have been expressed in strong terms as well

– **Lord Steyn** *(Deutsche Genossenschaftsbank v Burnhope)* - the construction found by the majority was "devoid of any redeeming commercial sense".

– *West Bromwich* - majority concluded that the phrase "Any claim (whether sounding in recission for undue influence or otherwise)was actually used by the parties to mean "Any claim sounding in recission (whether for undue influence or otherwise)".

– **Lord Lloyd -** Purposive interpretation was a useful tool where the purpose could be identified with reasonable certainty, but creative interpretation was not.

- **Lord Hoffman (majority) -** Rejected Lord Lloyd's analysis. It was perfectly acceptable for the court to interpret words in the way in which the parties must have understood them.

Uncertainty -

- Exclusion clauses and a clause in a contract - entitles a party to terminate a contract in certain circumstances, have traditionally been subjected to stricter rules of construction.

But...
Ex. British Fermentation Products Ltd v Compair Reavell Ltd [1999]
Ex. Ellis Tylin Ltd v Co-op Retail Services Ltd [1999]

- Judge Bowsher applied the *Investor Compensation Scheme* principles to the construction of an exclusion clause and a termination clause respectively

- Have the or are the old rules of interpretation about to be abandoned? (appear so)

Ex. Bank of Credit and Commerce International SA v Ali

- **Lord Hoffman -** "The disappearance of artificial rules for the construction of exemption clauses seems to me in accordance with the general trend in matters of construction which has been to try to assimilate judicial techniques of construction to those which would be used by a reasonable speaker of the language in the interpretation of any serious utterance in ordinary life"

- Commercial sense in purposive approach is applauded

- "A degree of uncertainty may turn out to be the price which has to be paid for the adoption of a more flexible, and hopefully fairer, approach to matters of construction" (McMeel)

1. Emphasis on the second principle ("factual matrix")

- Factual matrix seems to stem from Lord Wilberforce's speech in *Prenn v Simmonds [1971]*

- Criticism - "the counsel have wildly different ideas as to what a matrix is and what it includes".

- Lawyers may seek to exploit the breadth of the notion of "matrix of fact".

- Sir Christopher Staughton (1999) - "it is hard to imagine a ruling more calculated to perpetuate the vast cost of commercial litigation".

Lord Hoffman (Bank of Credit and Commerce International SA v Ali) responded to these criticisms:

- "I did not think it necessary to emphasise that I meant anything which a reasonable man would have regarded as relevant. I was merely saying that there is no conceptual limit to what can be regarded as background. It is not, for example, confined to the factual background but can include the state of law (as in cases in which one takes into account that the parties are unlikely to have intended to agree to something unlawful or legally ineffective)or proved common assumptions which were in fact quite mistaken... I was certainly not encouraging a trawl through "background" which could not have made a reasonable person think that the parties must have departed from conventional usage".

- Clear message: the factual matrix does have its limits

- The weight attributed to evidence derived from the background to the contract is likely to be less if issue focussed around standard contracts and industry norms. *(Re Sigma Finance Corp (in administrative receivership)[2009/10]*, or to a public document which is available for inspection *(Cherry Tree Investments Ltd v Landmain Ltd [2012]*

1. **Emphasis on the fourth and fifth principles**

- Fourth principle - emphasises the meaning of documents rather than the meaning of individual words and accepts parties do sometimes use the wrong words or syntax

- Used where there are badly drafted contracts (Multi-Link Leisure Developments v North Lanarkshire Council [2010] [2011]

– Principle 5 has been criticised, as it "is revolutionary because it overrode the previous understanding that, rectification apart, the court could not depart from the words of the document to find an agreement different from that stated in the document".

– It "confuses the meaning of what the parties said in the document with what they meant to say but did not say".

– "Close relationship" between interpretation and rectification, in that courts today can achieve results, which in previous generations would have been reached (if at all) via rectification *(Oceanbulk Shipping and Trading SA v TMT Asia Ltd [2010]*

– But this means modern courts willing to engage in a degree of re-writing the contract under the guise of interpretation; this can be described as, "corrective interpretation" (Arden LJ) (Cherry Tree Investments Ltd v Persimmon Homes Ltd [2009]

– Narrow confines

Lord Hoffmann (Chartbrook Ltd Persimmon Homes Ltd [2009]

– "It requires a strong case to persuade the court that something must have gone wrong with the language".

– Not likely a "Strong case" will be made by demonstrating that the contract is more favourable to one party.

– This does not show that something must have gone wrong with the language – it may merely mean one party has got a good deal while the other has not – very common.

– The court may, as in Chartbrook, conclude that the contract document does not mean what it says, and it will then adopt a construction which gives effect to the intention of the parties

Lord Hoffmann (Chartbrook)

– "No limit to the amount of red ink or verbal rearrangement or correction which the court is allowed".

– Court must be "clear that something has gone wrong with the language" and it must be "clear what a reasonable person would have understood the parties to have meant".

— Both the problems and issues need to be clear

— This dual requirement should limit uncertainty in Lord Hoffmann's fourth and fifth principles (Scottish Windows Fund and Life Assurance Society v BGC International [2012]

Rix LJ (ING Bank NV v Ros Roca SA [2011])

— "Judges should not see in *Chartbrook* an open sesame for reconstructing the parties' contract, but an opportunity to remedy by construction a clear error of language which could not have been intended", so that construction cannot be "pushed beyond its proper limits in pursuit of remedying what is perceived to be a flaw in the working of a contract"

1. The admissibility of evidence of pre-contractual negotiations and of conduct subsequent to the making of the contract

— Lord Hoffman did not refer to the latter in *Investors Compensation Scheme,* but did deal with the admissibility of evidence of pre-contractual negotiations in his third principle

— *Chartbrook* - direct challenge made to the rule that evidence of pre-contractual negotiations is *inadmissible*

— H of L affirmed the general rule that evidence of pre-contractual negotiations is inadmissible

— Certainty and need to avoid an unacceptable addition to the cost of litigation were driving factors here.

— **Lord Hoffmann** - "law of contract is designed to enforce promises with a high degree of predictability and the more one allows conventional meanings or syntax to be displaced by inferences drawn from background, the less predictable the outcome is likely to be".

— **Lord Rodger** - if general rule is to be changed, it should be "on the basis of a fully informed debate in a forum where the competing policies can be properly investigated and evaluated".

— In the absence of an intervention, the general rule excluding evidence of pre-contractual negotiations, is now firmly English contract law

Lord Hoffmann (Chartbrook) - addressing the scope of the rule

— "The rule excludes evidence of what was said or done during the course of negotiating the agreement for the purpose of drawing inferences about what the contract meant. It does not exclude the use of such evidence for other purposes: for example, **to establish that a fact which may be relevant as background was known to the parties or to support a claim for rectification or estoppel. These are not exceptions to the rule. They operate outside it**".

Lord Hoffmann provides for 3 situations which are outside the scope of the exclusionary clause

1. **A fact which may be relevant as background was known to the parties**

— Seems possible to refer to pre-contractual negotiations in so far as part of factual matrix

— Lord Clarke (Oceanbulk Shipping and Trading SA v TMT Asia Ltd) - factual matrix "may well include objective facts communicated by one party to the other in the course of negotiations".

— Distinction of admissible and inadmissible may not be clear.

Ex. Scottish Windows Fund and Life Assurance Society v BGC International [2012]

— Court was inclined admissibility

— Court of appeal decided not to rely upon pre-contractual negotiations to establish "the general object of the transaction" or as evidence of the "genesis and objective of the transaction".

— **Arden LJ** - "Judges should exercise considerable caution before treating as admissible communications in the course of pre-contractual negotiations relied on as evidencing the parties' objective aim in completing the transaction."

— **Davis LJ** - counsel for the respondents had looked too far into pre-contractual negotiations, "with a view to establishing a commercial objective which could re-fashion the wording", of the clause in issue, "away from its ostensibly plain meaning". This was not permissible.

1. **To support a claim for rectification**

– If the issue in front of court is one that relates to the interpretation, pre-contractual negotiations are inadmissible (even under Lord Hoffmann's fifth principle).

– But, if it relates to rectification of the contract, pre-contractual negotiations are admissible.

– Buxton -"all but the most negligent of counsel will plead rectification in order to be entitled to bring the pre-contractual materials before the court".

1. **To support a claim for estoppel**

– Pre-contractual negotiations are admissible to demonstrate or establish an estoppel.

– However, very difficult to successfully rely on an estoppel by convention, because the requirement that both parties entered into the contract on the basis of a common assumption.

– Generally, assumption would be a matter of dispute between the parties, if this is so, estoppel by convention cannot be established

– ING Bank NV v Ros Roca SA [2011] - exceptional case where estoppel by convention was invoked with success.

Evidence of conduct subsequent to the making of the contract is also inadmissible

– Reason is that contract could mean one thing when signed but mean something completely different after it was signed, by virtue of the conduct of the parties after the making of the contract (Schuler AG v Wickham Machine Tool Sales Ltd [1974]

– Latter rule limited to written contracts and will not apply to oral contracts, where evidence of conduct subsequent to the making of the contract is admissible (Maggs (t/a BM Builders) v Marsh [2006].

— Evidence of conduct subsequent to contracting may be relevant to a plea of estoppel and estoppel by convention (James Miller & Partners Ltd v Whitworth Street Estates (Manchester) Ltd [1970])(Mannai Investment Co Ltd v Eagle Star Life Insurance Co Ltd)

English law takes a narrow approach to the interpretation of contracts, 2 principle respects:

1. **English courts take a more literal approach to the interpretation of contracts.**

2. **Restricted range of materials is admissible in evidence in England, particularly the exclusion of pre-contractual negotiations and conduct subsequent to the making of the contract**

Rule of interpretation

— **Contra Proferentem** rule - ambiguity in a clause is interpreted against the party seeking to rely on it

Reinforced by regulation 7 of the Unfair Terms in Consumer Contracts Regulations 1999:

1. A seller or supplier shall ensure that any written term of a contract is expressed in plain, intelligible language

2. If there is doubt about the meaning of a written term, the interpretation most favourable to the consumer shall prevail...

Rectification

— Once contract has been interpreted, party can argue the written agreement, as interpreted, does not reflect the agreement reached.

— Court may be asked to rectify the document… to ensure it reflects the agreements.

Ex. Lovell & Christmas Ltd v Wall (1911)

- Claimant asked court to interpret a contract in a specific way.

- This failed, so claimant tried to have the contract document rectified

- Fine line between **interpretation and rectification**

- **Interpretation** - ascribing a meaning to terms

- **Rectification** - the meaning of a document has already been ascertained, and this document is then rectified to better give effect to the intention of the parties

Ex. Nittan (UK) Ltd v Solent Steel Fabrication Ltd (1981)

- Court of Appeal read "Sargrove Electronic Contracts Ltd" as if it read "Sargrove Automation".

- This *avoided the need to rectify the document*

Corrective interpretation

- Courts have applied Lord Hoffmann's restatement of principles.

- Fourth and fifth principles - Arden LJ described as "corrective interpretation" *(Cherry Tree Investments Ltd v Landmain Ltd (2012)*

- Provides courts with more flexibility to conclude that the parties have used the wrong words to give effect to their intention – this avoids the need to formally rectify.

- A court can use "corrective interpretation", where parties make a mistake of language or syntax.

- But "corrective interpretation" not appropriate if the parties have not provided for a particular circumstance or have omitted a particular clause in error. *(Cherry Tree Investments Ltd v Landmain Ltd)*

- Rectification then becomes the most appropriate course of action.

Rectification is a remedy which is concerned with defects in the recording, of a contract – this contrasts with a defect in the making of a contract.

Ex. Frederick E Rose (London) Ltd v William H Pim Jnr & Co Ltd (1953)

Facts

- Claimants asked to supply quantity of "Moroccan horse beans known here as feveroles".

- Claimants didn't understand the term feveroles,

- They asked the defendants what it meant, and they replied stating they were simply horsebeans.

- Parties entered into a contract; defendants would supply to the claimants some horsebeans

- Both parties believed that horsebeans were feveroles when making the agreement.

- Became known that feveroles were a more expensive variety horsebean.

- The people the claimant supplied claimed damages from the claimants on the ground that the horsebeans which had been supplied to them were not feveroles.

- Claimants sought the contract with the defendants rectified, to include insertion of the word feveroles

Judgement

- Court of Appeal refused

- Document had recorded the intention of the parties

- Parties under a shared misapprehension.

Rectification as an equitable discretionary remedy

- Based on discretion of the court

- Gradually courts have been more willing to use.

Considerations before deciding whether to rectify a document (by the court)

Court will only rectify a document where...

1. **Convincing proof that document fails to accurately record the intention of the parties**

Joscelyne v Nissen (1970), George Wimpey UK Ltd v VI Components Ltd (2005)

— Because of certainty, need a lot of proof. (the Olympic Pride 1980)

— Objective test in determining common intention. *(Chartbrook Ltd v Persimmon Homes Ltd [2009])*

— Although it is stated that "some subjective evidence of intention or understanding" is usually required in a rectification claim, this is because party seeking rectifications needs to demonstrate that he did make the relevant mistake at the time of entry into the contract *(Daventry District Council v Daventry & District Housing Ltd [2011]*

1. **The document must fail to record the intention of both parties**
Unilateral mistake not sufficient to base a claim to rectification (Riverlate Properties v Paul [1975])

— If one party mistakenly believes the document correctly expresses the parties' common intention, while other party is aware of mistake, rectification may be available (A Roberts and Co Ltd v Leicestershire CC [1961]

— *unconscionable conduct* may give claimant entitlement to rectification.

Ex. Commission for the New Towns v Cooper (Great Britain) [1995] (unconscionable conduct)

— **Stuart-Smith LJ** - "where A intends B to be mistaken as to the construction of the agreement, so conducts himself that he diverts B's attention from discovering the mistake by making false and misleading statements, and B, in fact, makes the very mistake that A intends, then notwithstanding that A does not actually know, but merely suspects, that B is mistaken, and it cannot be shown that the mistake was induced by any mis-representation, rectification may be granted"

— Mere existence of even a serious mistake, will not allow party to seek rectification of the contract

— Need to prove that the other party to the contract knew of the mistake so that it can be said to have behaved dishonestly or unconscionable (George Wimpey UK Ltd v VI Components Ltd [2005]

1. **The document must have been preceded either by a con-cluded contract or by a "continuing common intention"**

— Generally straightforward if there is a previously enforceable contract.

— More difficult if there has been simply a "common continuing intention in regard to a particular provision or aspect of the agreement" (Crane v Hegeman-Harris [1970])

— "the continuing common intention" is tricky. This needs to be accompanied by evidence of "an outward expression of ac-cord.

Ex. Joscelyne v Nissen [1970]
Facts

— Father and daughter agreed daughter would purchase father's company

— She would pay all the expenses of the father's home, including gas, electricity and coal bills in return for purchase.

— The formal contract did not mention the daughter's agreement to pay these bills

Judgement

— There was no prior contract to which the court could investi-gate.

— Was sufficient evidence of a continuing common intention that the daughter pays the gas, electricity and coal bills

— *Rectification won't be granted in favour of a claimant who has been guilty of excessive delay in seeking rectification, nor will it be granted against a bona fide purchaser for value without notice*

Implied terms

— Courts may be prepared to hold that other terms must be implied into the contract.

Such terms may be implied from one of three sources
The source of implied terms is terms implied by....

Statute

— Parliament has seen fit in many instances, to imply terms into contracts

— Based on public policy – rather than intention of parties.

— Example of statutorily implied terms is **Sections 12-15 of the Sale of Goods Act 1979:**

— **s 12 (1)** - it is an implied condition of a contract for the sale of goods that the seller has the right to sell the goods

— **s 12 (2)** - there is an implied warranty that the goods are free from charges or incumbrances in favour of third parties

— **s 13 (1)** - there is also an implied condition that goods sold by description shall correspond with the description

— **s 15** - goods sold by sample shall correspond with the sample

— **s 14 (2)** - in the case of a seller who sells goods in the course of a business, there is an implied condition that the goods supplied under the contract are of satisfactory quality

— **s 14 (2C)** - except in relation to defects drawn to the buyer's attention before the contract was concluded or, in the case where the buyer examines the goods, as regards defects which that examination ought to reveal

— **s 14 (3)** - where the seller sells goods in the course of a business and the buyer makes known to the seller any particular purpose for which the goods are being bought, there is an implied condition that the goods supplied under the contract are reasonably fit for that purpose

Custom

— Contract could be found to incorporate a relevant custom of the market, trade or locality in which the contract is made *(Hutton v Warren (1836)*

— Unless, this custom is inconsistent with the express terms of the contract *(Palgrave, Brown & Son Ltd v SS Turid (owners) [1922])*

— Must be shown such a custom was generally accepted by those doing business in the particular trade in the particular place *(Kum v Wah Tat Bank Ltd [1971])*

Common law

There are **two types** *of terms which are applied at common law:*

— *Implied in fact*

— The idea that the term is being implied as a matter of fact

— *Implied in law*

— These are implied into all contracts of a type

— Terms implied in law are not as directly related to the intention of parties.

— Hence the terms are frequently implied into contracts such as employment or leases, not because of the relationship between the particular parties, but as a result of a more general set of rules governing the relationship of employer and employee or landlord and tenant

— The test which must be satisfied before a term will be implied into a contract is the subject of some *controversy*

— Lord Hoffmann's Judgement *(A-G of Belize v Belize Telecom Ltd [2009])*, where he tried to re-state the law relating to the implication of terms (similar to his restatement of the principles by which contracts are interpreted in *(Investors Compensation Scheme Ltd v Wes Bromwich Building Society [1998])*

60

— *"Implication of a term is an exercise in the construction of the contract as a whole"*

The court is concerned only to discover what the instrument means...

— "It follows that in every case in which it is said that some provision ought to be implied in an instrument, the question for the court is whether such a provision would spell out in express words what the instrument, read against the relevant background, would reasonably be understood to mean... There is only one question: is that what the instrument, read as a whole against the relevant background, would reasonably be understood to mean?"

— A court which needs to interpret the express words of a contract does not normally have difficulty in identifying the term which it is called to interpret

— The courts task is to ascertain the meaning of the words which the parties have used

— But a court which is asked to imply a term into a contract, must identify and formulate the term which is to be implied into the contract

— Uncertainty rests on the relationship between Lord Hoffmann's approach and that taken by courts in previous cases

Tests

Officious bystander test

— "Prima facie that which in any contract is left to be implied and need not be expressed is something so obvious that it goes without saying; so that, if, while the parties were making their bargain an officious bystander were to suggest some express provision for it in the agreement, they would testify suppress him with a common, "Oh, of course" *(MacKinnon LJ in Shirlaw v Southern Foundries Ltd [1939])*

— Thus, the implication must be "necessary to give the transaction such business efficacy as the parties must have intended" (The Moorcock 1889)

Lord Simon (BP Refinery (Westernport) Pty Ltd v Shire of Hastings (1978), summarised these tests in the following terms:

For a term to be implied, the following conditions (which may overlap) must be satisfied:

1. Must be reasonable and equitable

2. Necessary to give business efficacy to the contract

3. So obvious "it goes without saying"

4. Capable of close expression

5. Cannot contradict any express term of the contract

- Lord Hoffmann (A-G of Belize) - this summary is "best regarded, not as a series of independent tests which must each be surmounted, but rather as a collection of different ways in which the judges have tried to express the central idea that the proposed implied term must spell out what the contract actually means, or in which they have explained why they did not think that it did so"

- These traditional tests should not be regarded as "different or additional tests".

- Instead, they should be seen as different ways of expressing the essential nature of the test to be applied, namely that... "the effect of the implication must be to make the instrument mean what it would reasonably be understood to mean" *(Stena Line Ltd v Merchant Navy Ratings Pension Fund Trustees Ltd [2011])*

Lord Clarke agreed with this view (Mediterranean Salvage & Towage Ltd v Seamar Trading & Commerce Inc (The Reborn) [2009])

- Lord Hoffmann was "not in any way resiling from the often stated proposition that it must be necessary to imply the proposed term. It is never sufficient that it should be reasonable".

- Court does not have power to imply a term into a contract simply because it is reasonable to do so

- Lord Denning has advocated this *(Liverpool CC v Irwin [1976])*

- But this was rejected by the H of L, who insisted that "the term must be a necessary one before it will be implied"*(Hughes v Greenwich London BC [1994])*

- Courts are also reluctant to imply a term where the parties have entered into a carefully drafted written document: here, court is likely to find that the written contract constitutes a complete agreement (Shell UK Ltd v Lostock Garages Ltd [1976])

- Lord Simon (BP Refinery (Westernport) Pty Ltd v Shire of Hastings) - term will not be implied into a contract if it would be inconsistent with the express wording of the contract (Duke of Westminster v guild [1985])

- Judgement of Lord Hoffmann in *(A-G of Belize)*, is directed to the implication of terms as a matter of fact *(Geys v Societe Generale, London Branch [2012])*

- Doesn't directly relate to terms implied as a matter of law

So what test do courts apply when deciding whether to imply a term into a contract as a matter of law?

- Test reflects the court's perception of the nature of the relationship between the parties.

Lord Bridge (Scally v Southern Health and Social Services Board)

- "a clear distinction between the search for an implied term necessary to give business efficacy to a particular contract and the search, *based on wider consideration,* for a term which the law will imply as a necessary incident of a definable category of contractual relationship".

- These "wider considerations" have proved hard to recognise... however:

Dyson LJ (Crossley v Faithful & Gould Holdings Ltd [2004]

- Courts ought not "focus on the elusive concept of necessity" which is "somewhat protean" but rather "Should recognise that, to some extent at least, the existence and scope of standardised implied terms raise questions of reasonableness, fairness, and the balancing of competing policy considerations".

— Principal issue — *"whether or not there was an implied term of any contract of employment that the employer will take reasonable care for the economic well-being of his employee"*

— Court of Appeal refused to make the implication

— Court of Appeal - "such an implied term would impose an unfair and unreasonable burden on the employers".

— Interests of employers and employees can and do conflict — it was held that it would be "unreasonable", to force the employer "to have regard to the employee's financial circumstances when he takes lawful business decisions which may affect the employee's economic welfare".

— It was held not to be the function of an employer to "act as his employee's financial adviser", and there were "no obvious policy reasons to impose on an employer the general duty to protect his employee's economic well being"

5. The Classification of Contractual Terms

Summary

- The terms of a contract are important in the context of breaches of contract.
- The traditional classification of terms rests on the distinction between important, central terms known as conditions and minor complimentary terms known as warranties.
- However, this distinction is not always clear.
- The court in Hong Kong Fir Shipping Co v Kawasaki Kisen Kaisha Ltd developed a further category of innominate terms. The breach of these terms do not always give rise to a right to termination, or necessarily confine remedies to damages. Instead, the court is flexible to assess the impact of the breach.
- An inherent conflict is present in classifying terms between certainty and fairness.

The classification of terms

Contractual terms vary in their importance. This variance is recognised by contract law through the use of conditions and warranties in contracts.

- **Condition** – an essential term of the contract, something of great importance that 'goes to the root' of the agreement.
- **Warranty** – a less important term of a contract.

The classification of terms as conditions or warranties becomes important when a breach occurs
Breach of a **condition** - entitles the innocent party (IP) to:

1. Terminate performance of contract and obtain damages for loss, **or**

2. Affirm contract and recover damages

Breach of a **warranty** – only entitles IP to:

1. Claim damages, cannot terminate the contract.

Distinguishing between a condition and warranty

A term can be classified as a condition by statute, judicial interpretation or by classification from the parties.

Statutory classification

- An example of statutory classification can be seen in Section 12-15 of the Sale of Goods Act 1979.

- These sections classify these implied terms to be conditions. For example, implied terms as to fitness for purpose and compliance with description are held to be conditions.

Judicial classification

- **The courts may also find terms to be conditions. This can be achieved through two different grounds:**

Performance of term 'goes to the root' of the contract

- It can be implied that the parties must have intended for this term to be a condition.

- Breach of this type of term would entitle IP to treat themselves as being discharged (Couchman v Hill 1947).

- Courts, in determining the importance of a term, will consider the commercial context.

- Kerr LJ - "court is making in effect a value judgement about the commercial significance of the term in question" (State Trading Corp of India Ltd v M Golodetz Ltd 1989)

Binding authority requires court to hold term is a condition

- Where parties in a particular industry trade on standard terms the courts will follow authority on classification.

- Governing factor is the need for certainty within an industry.

- Prioritising certainty does though mean parties can be entitled to terminate contracts despite suffering no loss.
  Ex. Arcos Ltd v E A Ronaasen & Son 1933

- Timber was described and sold as being half an inch thick.

- The timber was bought to be used in making cement barrels

- Timber delivered was 9/16-inch-thick, this did not render its usefulness in making the cement barrels void.

- The buyer was held to be entitled to reject the timber. Their motivation for doing so was not borne out of hardship, rather the price of timber had fallen.

- This case, therefore, demonstrates that the courts are not concerned with the real reasons for termination.

- Parties need only possess the right to terminate, rather than real, good faith reasons to terminate a contract.

- This approach is favoured for reasons of certainty. The task of finding the 'real reason' for termination would also be costly and difficult.

Classification of the parties

- If contract states that particular term is a condition then, term will be regarded as a condition.

Ex. Lombard North Central plc v Butterworth 1987

- In a contract hiring out computers, a clause was included stating it was the essence of the contract that the hirer should pay each instalment quickly.

- In fact, the hirer failed to pay for some instalments promptly.

- The owners regained possession of their computers and sued for damages.

- The Court of Appeal held the failure to pay a single instalment promptly was sufficiently important to repudiate the contract.

— Court places no restriction upon the right of the parties to classify the relative importance of the term of their contract.

The courts must be sure the parties actually intended for the word 'condition' to be interpreted in the technical, legal sense.
Ex. Schuler AG v Wickham Machine Tool Sales Ltd (1974)

— As part of a distribution agreement it was stated, "it shall be a condition of this agreement that Wickham shall send its representatives to visit (6 named UK manufacturers) at least once in every week for the purpose of soliciting orders".

— Wickham failed to make some visits to named manufacturers across the 4-year contract.

— Schuler claimed because of this failure it was entitled to terminate agreement as Wickham had broken condition of the agreement

Lord Reid

— The use of the word 'condition' should not be treated as "conclusive evidence" of an intention to treat terms as conditions in the technical way.

— Would though provide strong evidence.

— The more unreasonable the consequences of treating a term as a condition in its technical sense, the less likely that the parties intended to use the word condition in that way.

— He felt finding this term to be a condition was extremely unreasonable.

— Lord Reid was compelled to interpret "condition", in its non-technical sense

Lord Wilberforce

— Dissented and found the term was a condition.

— The majority approach assumed, "Contrary to the evidence, that both parties... adopted a standard of easy-going tolerance, rather than one of aggressive, insistent punctuality and efficiency".

Schuler has been described as the 'high water mark' of the courts' reluctance to classify terms as conditions, despite the use of the word in contracts. (Heritage Oil and Gas v Tullow Uganda Ltd [2014 EWCA Civ 1048).

– Crucial both parties agree to classification of a term before term is given the status of a condition.

– Position is different when one party *serves a notice* on the other party, hoping to make performance of a particular obligation, "the essence of the contract".

Two issues

1. Entitlement of IP to serve such a notice

– IP entitled to serve such a notice as right to give notice is not confined to essential terms of the contract but can be exercised in relation to any term of the contract (Behzadi v Shaftesbury Hotels Ltd 1992)

– Notice can be served at moment of breach.

– Period of notice must be reasonable

1. The effect of the notice
Ex. Re Olympia & York Canary Warf Ltd (1933)

– Morritt J - rejected that failure to comply with "time of the essence notice" argument, was not in itself a sufficient basis to constitute repudiation of the contract

– This is correct, as if failure to comply would amount to repudiation, then one party would be given unilateral party to turn non-essential term into an essential term.

Ex. Samarenko v Dawn Hill House Ltd (2011)

– Rix LJ - serving of a notice making time of the essence of the contract, cannot impose an additional obligation on the recipient

- Hence when underlying term broken is a warranty, then unilateral giving of notice purporting to make time of the essence, cannot turn warranty into a condition

Fundamental importance here is whether or not the parties **together agreed** upon a classification.

The need for change?

Cases show the primary feature of determining classification has been the importance of the term as opposed to the consequences that flow from a breach.
Notably, in *Arcos Ltd v E A Ronaasen & Son*, a term has been classified as a condition, despite insignificant consequences resulting from its breach.

Justification

1. Freedom of parties to classify.
2. **Certainty** in commercial transactions.

Certainty

- Certainty can be achieved through classifying a term based on its importance.

- However, uncertainty can arise, when determining whether the term which has been broken is actually a condition

- In *The Naxos (1990)*, the majority of the HoL held that obligation of the seller to have the cargo ready for delivery at any time within the contract period was a condition. The Court of Appeal had previously found the term not to be a condition.

- This uncertainty is limited to previously unclassified terms.

Change to make critical factor the consequence of breach:

- This would remove the injustices of cases in which the real reason for termination is not connected with the breach of the term.

- Then IP would only be entitled to terminate the performance of the contract if the consequences of the breach were sufficiently serious *(Boone v Eyre 1777 and Behn V Burness 1863)*

– A trade-off again occurs here with certainty.

Criticism of classifying term as a condition

In classifying terms as conditions too readily, there is a risk that parties are being encouraged to terminate contracts, rather than continue performance – the very nature of a contract.
Ex. The Hansa Nord (1976)

- "In principle, contracts are made to be performed and not to be avoided according to the whims of market fluctuation, and where there is a free choice between 2 possible constructions I think the court should tend to prefer that construction which will ensure performance, and not encourage avoidance of contractual obligations"(Roskill LJ)

- Similar to the Arcos v Ronaasen case, the buyer was searching for a means of avoiding a bad bargain. Real reason question again prevalent.

- In cases such as these, performance is more likely where a term is not classified as a condition.

Benefit of classifying term as a condition

- Classification of term as condition can give an incentive to a potential contract-breaker to perform their obligations.

- Under this analysis, classification of term as a condition can act as an incentive to performance rather than termination

- This argument is not convincing. A more important consideration when thinking about reform should be the injustices caused by termination in cases such as Arcos v Ronaasen.

Conflict of certainty v Justice/fairness

- **Certainty** - focus on the nature of the term broken, rigid approach to remedies.

- **Justice** - focus on the breach, and its consequences. Flexible approach to remedies.

How to balance these demands

1. Statutory restriction upon the right of the buyer to reject goods

Section 15A Sale of Goods Act 1979 Subsection 1 (Sale and Supply of Goods Act 1994)

- "Where the buyer would have the right to reject goods by reason of a breach on the part of the seller of a term implied by sections 13 to 15 of the Sale of Goods Act 1979, but the breach is so slight that it would be unreasonable for him to reject them, then, if the buyer does not deal as consumer, the breach is not to be treated as a breach of a condition, but may be treated as a breach of a warranty"

- Hence buyer would be confined to claiming damages

- Seller has to show that the breach is slights as to preclude the buyer from rejecting the goods

- However, everything hinges on the word **"slight"**

Limitations of the word slight

- Treitel (Arcos v Ronaasen) - "the difference between half an inch and 9/16 of an inch is by no means obviously slight".

- If it is not slight, then the buyer is not deprived of his right to reject regardless of how unreasonable his decision to reject would be

- Only applies to a breach by the seller of one of the terms implied by Sections 13-15 (1979)

- Has no application...

- To a breach by the seller of Section 12 of the Act

- To the breach of an express term of the contract

- To the sellers right to terminate following a breach by the buyer

- Only applies where buyer is not a consumer

- Consumer buyer not to be deprived of his right to reject the goods

- Not to be confined to a claim in damages because damages are unlikely to be an adequate remedy for a purchaser who has not bought with a view to reselling the goods

- Hence new provision only applies in commercial context

- This is strange as provision reduces certainty at the point it is needed most

Attempts made to preserve certainty

- Enacting new restriction shall apply "unless a contrary intention appears in, or is to be implied from the contract" (s15 A (2))

- The meaning here is not obvious, intended to exclude from the reform clauses such as time clauses where it is generally accepted that breach should give right to terminate.

- The effect of this reform is to take away a degree of certainty in commercial transactions but limit to which it is subject (exclusion of seller termination following buyer breach), makes it hard to resist conclusion of Treitel, "the section has sacrificed certainty without attaining justice".

3. Focusing attention on the consequences of the breach

- Remedial flexibility

- Understanding that finding a distinction between conditions and warranties can be difficult.

Innominate Terms

Ex. Hong Kong Fir Shipping Co Ltd v Kawasaki Kisen Kaisha Ltd (1962)
Diplock LJ - "There are many contractual undertakings.... which cannot be categorised as being "conditions" or "warranties"... Of such undertakings, all that can be predicated is that some breaches will, and others will not give rise to an event which will deprive the party, not in default of substantially the whole benefit which it was intended that he should obtain".

Innominate term distinguished from condition and warranty

- Breach of innominate term does not automatically give right to terminate(condition).

- Innocent party is not confined to damages (warranty).

But remedial flexibility can be problematic....

- Uncertainty over right to terminate.

- *Courts will have regard to all relevant circumstances of the case when deciding whether the breach was of a sufficiently serious character:*

Carter (2012) factors relied upon by the court:

1. Any detriment caused, or likely to be caused, by the breach

2. Any delay caused, or likely to be caused, by the breach

3. The value of any performance received by or tendered to the party not in breach

4. The cost of making any performance given or tendered by the party in breach conform with the requirements of the contract

5. Any opportunity enjoyed by the party in breach to remedy the discrepancies in its performance

6. The consequences of any prior breach of the contract by the party in breach and whether further breaches were a likely consequence of the breach at issue

7. Whether the party not in breach will be adequately compensated by an award of damages in respect of the breach

- Highly dependent on facts of the case.

High cost of uncertainty:

- If contracting party is wrong and tries to terminate, when they are not entitled to do so, they themselves will now be held to have repudiated their obligations under contract and may be liable to pay substantial damages.

− This new category of innominate terms creates further difficulty in distinguishing between innominate term, condition, and warranty.

Interests of certainty and justice

− Fairness: favours classifications of terms as innominate terms, a remedy can be tailored to facts of the case

− Certainty: favours classification as a condition, because remedial consequences will be clear

− Must balance these competing interests.

− Balancing exercise - requires court to balance competing policy considerations in line with facts of case.

− However, Courts have engaged in such a balancing exercise:

− *Ex. BS & N Ltd (BVI) v Micado Shipping Ltd (Malta) (The Seaflower) (2001)*

− Atkins J - term between parties was an innominate term, but Court of Appeal held it as a condition

Courts have been reluctant to find that a term is a condition unless strong evidence to support this conclusion.

− *Ex. Bunge Corp v Tradax Export SA (1981)*

− H of L – Key is whether term is "of the essence of the contract".

− Lord Wilberforce - "the courts should not be too ready to interpret contractual clauses as conditions".

− Despite commercially vital terms where the need for certainty is greatest, greater consideration will be given to interests of "justice", by classifying contract terms as innominate terms

− This will give courts flexibility in granting appropriate relief

Ex. Hansa Nord (1976) and Arcos Ltd v E A Ronaasen &Son (1933)

− Buyer of shipment attempted to reject cargo due failure to make delivery 'in good condition'.

— Despite initial price of cargo - £100,000, buyers managed to purchase same cargo for just £30,000 on the grounds of the reduced quality.

— Buyers used citrus pulp for originally intended purpose.

— COA - term broken was not a condition but an innominate term, applying *Hong Kong Fir*, the court concluded that consequences of breach were not sufficiently serious.

— Buyers, therefore, confined to a claim in damages to reflect loss in value of cargo caused by its defective state.

6. Exclusion Clauses

- **Exclusion clause -** "clause in a contract or a term in a notice which appears to exclude or restrict a liability or a legal duty which would otherwise arise" (Yates 1982)

Exclusion clauses can come in *different forms;*

- Exclusion of liability when contract breached

- Negligence

- Limiting damages to a specified sum

- **Indemnity clause** – promise of reimbursement for liability incurred in the performance of contract.

Exclusion clauses: defence or definition?

Exclusion clause example

- Paul wants to have his furniture moved to a new house.

- Paul contracts with Steve to move furniture, a self-employed tradesman who has no insurance.

- Steve relies on owner's using their own insurance policies.

- Steve inserts a clause in the contract stating, 'no liability accepted for damage, however, caused while this contract is performed'.

2 views about function of clause:

1. **This defines the obligations of the parties.**

- Steve accepted a limited obligation to transmit the goods, without accepting an obligation to become liable on damage.

1. **Traditionally, clause acts a defence for a party in breach**

- Failure to deliver goods safely constitutes a breach.

– The role of the exclusion clause is to give Steve a defence to Paul's claim for breach.

Serious difficulties with traditional view:

– Steve simply has not accepted an absolute duty to deliver Paul's goods. It could only be held he had if the exclusion clause was not considered.

– Why ignore the exclusion clause? It surely must form part of Steve's offer to Paul and therefore part of the obligations undertaken.

– No justification for ignoring the exclusion clause.

– If exclusion clauses are instead treated as merely one means of defining obligations, any justification for subjecting exclusion clauses to separate regulations disappears.

– Merely a term parties accept in contracting.

Adams and Brownsword (1988) attack this conception that exclusion clauses define agreement:

– "It is elegantly formalistic... and it ignores both the historical development of the problem and the realities of the situation".

– "Historical development" – referring to standard form contracts and the increase in exclusion clauses.

– "realities" referring to the fact that these standard form contracts are presented without any intention of negotiation of terms, or on a "take it or leave it basis". Affecting weaker, vulnerable party.

– Clauses just limit rights of weaker parties.

– Submitted, the evil here is not exclusion clauses, but instead the existence of *unfair terms.*

– Other doctrines can deal with this?

BUT... Courts and parliament generally treat exclusion clauses as a defence to a breach of an obligation.

The functions of exclusion clauses

1. **Allocation of risks**

In first example, the fact that a risk is clearly placed on one party avoids the need for both to insure against the same loss. More efficient.

1. **Reduce litigation costs through increased clarity**

2. **Used in standard form contracts to reduce negotiation costs.**

Socially harmful functions

— Exploits weaker party

— This may explain the caution which courts have treated exclusion clauses with.

An outline of the law

Use of exclusion clause in a contract must overcome 3 obstacles

1. Exclusion clause must be shown to be properly incorporated in contract

2. Must be clear that clause covers the loss which has arisen

3. No other rule of law to invalidate the exclusion clause

— First two more important historically

— Although at common law the court has power to strike down contract terms which are "contrary to public policy", no power to find exclusion clauses invalid because they were unreasonable.

— **Lord Denning** *(Gillespie Bros v Roy Bowles ltd [1973])* — courts construed parties to not have meant to contract on terms which were unreasonable.

— Courts now have statutory power under **UCTA (Unfair Contract Terms Act 1977)** - to control exclusion clauses — less need to use obstacles 1 and 2 to limit unreasonable terms.

– Expected focus will switch to the third stage

Incorporation

– Must be shown that exclusion clause was validly incorporated in contract.

Construction of exclusion clauses

– Need to show clause covers damages caused.

– Exclusion clauses interpreted differently to ordinary terms; more rigorously or restrictively

– Strict interpretation against the party trying to rely on it

– This is called the *contra* **proferentem rule** - ambiguity resolved against the party seeking to rely on exclusion clause.

– *"Proferens"* – party seeking to rely on clause, don't need to have imposed clause. (*Scottish Special Housing Association v Wimpey Construction UK Ltd [1986]*)

Consequence of contra proferentem rule

Draftsmen tried to evade the restrictive interpretations adopted in the courts

Ex. Wallis, Son and Wells v Pratt and Haynes [1911]

Facts

– Contract for the sale of seeds had clause that said sellers gave "no warranty express or implied" as to the description of the seeds

– Seeds different to description, so the buyers brought an action for damages against the sellers, who sought to rely on the exclusion clause.

Judgement

– Held couldn't rely on clause. Only covered breach of a warranty and, in failing to provide seeds which correspond with the description, the sellers had broken a condition (distinction between warranty and condition)

Impact seen in *Andrews Bros (Bournemouth) Ltd v Singer and Co Ltd [1934]*

- The *exclusion clause* stated that - "All conditions, warranties, and liabilities implied by statute, common law or otherwise are excluded".

Judgement

- **Greer LJ** - defendants were trying to escape the effect of Wallis, although they had included the word "condition" - they had not included word "express".

- Court held that the defendants had broken an express term of the contract – not excluded.

- Dangerous practice to rely upon a clause which states that "*the seller gives no warranty express or implied*"... or that "*the goods are not warranted free from defect*"...

- Includes a breach of a condition

Dangers provided by decision of COA in *KG Bominflot Bunkergesellschaft Fur Mineralole mnH & Co v Petroplus Marketing AG [2010]*

- Words "no guarantees, warranties or representations, express or implied, merchantability, fitness or suitability of the oil" - were held not to be effective to exclude liability for breach of the implied condition that goods be of satisfactory quality.

- No rule of law which requires the use of the word "condition" in order to exclude liability for breach of a condition

- In each case, question of construction of the particular clause.

- Safest way to contract remains to make express reference to the exclusion of liability for breach of a condition if this is the intention.

Stricter approach?
Ailsa Craig Fishing Co Ltd v Malvern Fishing Co Ltd [1983]

— H of L - held that in the case of limitation clauses, the *contra proferentem rule* didn't apply with the same rigour as in the case of exclusion clauses

— **Lord Fraser and Lord Wilberforce** - limitation clauses not viewed with the same hostility as exclusion clauses because of their role in risk allocation and more likely to be agreement between parties.

Objection - ignores the risk allocation function of exclusion clauses and assumption of agreement.
Ex. Evans LJ (BHP Petroleum Ltd v British Steel plc [2000])

— "I think it is unfortunate if the present authorities cannot be reconciled on the basis that no categorization is necessary and of a general rule that the more extreme the consequences are, in terms of excluding or modifying the liability which would otherwise arise, then the more stringent the Court's approach should be in requiring that the exclusion or limit should be clearly and unambiguously expressed. Indeed, if the requirement is of a clear and unambiguous provision, then it is not easy to see why degrees of clarity and lack of unambiguity should be recognized".

— Preferable approach which avoids rigid categorisation and instead uses a sliding-scale

— However, distinction between a limitation clause and an exclusion clause remains part of English law, *Alisa Craig* followed by H of L in *George Mitchell (Chesterhall) Ltd v Finney Lock Seeds Ltd [1983]*

Different approaches?
Ex. Photo Production Ltd v Securicor Transport Ltd [1980]

— **Lord Diplock** - "the reports are full of cases in which what would appear to be very strained constructions have been placed upon exclusion clauses".

— Lord Diplock said many cases involved consumer contracts, and "any need for this kind of judicial distortion of the English language has been banished by Parliament's having made these kinds of contract subject to the **Unfair Contract Terms Act 1977"**.

Lord Hoffmann (Bank of Credit and Commerce International SA v Ali [2001])

— Lord Hoffmann adopted a similar approach when he stated that:

— "The lesson which I would draw from the development of the rules for construing exemption clauses is that the judicial creativity, bordering on judicial legislation, which the application of that doctrine involved is a desperate remedy, to be invoked only if it is necessary to remedy a widespread injustice. Otherwise, there is much to be said for giving effect to what on ordinary principles of construction the parties agreed"

— *Contra proferentem* rule wasn't doubted in *Photo Production and BCCI v Ali*

— In both cases, the court was saying that it will operate only in cases of genuine ambiguity and that in future exclusion clauses should be given a more natural construction

2 situations remain where particular rules of construction are employed by the courts.

Where…

1. A party tries to exclude liability for his own **negligence**

2. He attempts to exclude liability for a **"fundamental breach"**

Negligence liability

— UCTA - provides severe restrictions on the ability to exclude liability for your own negligence.

— Courts view it as intuitively unlikely that parties will agree on this.

— Courts have evolved **3 specific rules of construction** (originated from the speech of Lord Morton of Henryton - *Canada Steamship Lines Ltd v The King 1952])*

1. **If a clause contains language which expressly exempts the party relying on the exclusion clause from the consequences of his own negligence then (subject to UCTA) effect must be given to the clause**

– Can use words such as "any act, omission, neglect or default" (synonym for negligence) to meet the required standard. *(Smith v UBM Chrysler (Scotland) Ltd 1978) (Monarch Airlines Ltd v London Luton Airport Ltd [1998])*

– Easiest to use words "negligence expressly".

– "loss whatsoever or howsoever occasioned" doesn't count. *(Shell Chemicals UK Ltd v P&O Roadtanks Ltd [1995])*

– If the first rule isn't satisfied the court will then proceed to apply the second and third rules

– While the first rule stands alone, the second and third rules constitute a double hurdle which must be overcome by a clause which fails to satisfy the first rule

1. **Consideration of whether the words are wide enough, in their ordinary meaning, to cover negligence**

– Doubt resolved against the party relying on the clause

– Exclusion clauses which have been held wide enough to satisfy this test include clauses which exclude liability for "any act or omission" or "any damage whatsoever".

1. **Consider whether exclusion clause may cover some kind of liability other than negligence**

– If related to other liability, courts will normally confine it and will be held not to extend to negligently inflicted loss

– Used to be that mere existence of a possible alternative source of liability would mean the clause could not cover negligence...

– Reconsidered by COA in *The Raphael [1982]*

Ex. The Raphael [1982]

— Where the alternative source of liability was "fanciful or remote" – existence wouldn't prevent the exclusion clause covering negligence

— If other source of liability realistic for the parties to intend the clause to apply to that other source of liability, does this mean that the clause cannot apply to negligence?

— **Stephenson J** - agreed with this

— **Lord Donaldson and May LJ** - clause would generally be interpreted as not excluding liability for negligence (matter of construction)

Combination of 2nd and 3rd rules can produce results which are unsatisfactory and contrary to the intention of the parties
2 problems can be identified

1. **Two rules make contradictory demands of the draftsmen**

— Second rule demands that clause be drafted widely while third rule asks for clause to be narrow, because the wider it is, the more likely it is that it will encompass other sources of liability.

1. **The parties may intend the same clause to apply both to negligently inflicted damage and to non-negligently inflicted damage**

Ex. Schenker & Co (Aust) Pty Ltd v Malpas Equipment and Services Pty Ltd [1990]

— **McGarvie J** - Canada Steamship approach was inconsistent with the more natural and ordinary rules of construction adopted by High Court of Australia in *Darlington Futures v Delco Australia Pty Ltd (1987)*

Departure from strained rules of construction as justified on the following ground:

— "To construe commercial contracts as they would be understood by business people serves primary aims of both the law and commerce. The law serves the community best if citizens understand it and are able to resolve their dispute themselves by reference to it, without resorting to lawyers or courts".

– Not yet English law approach.

– Some affirmation of the *Canada Steamship* rules in robust terms

Ex. Hobhouse J (EE Caledonia Ltd v Orbit Valve Co Europe [1993]

– "It has to be borne in mind that commercial contracts are drafted by parties with access to legal advice and in the context of established legal principles as reflected in the decisions of the courts. Principles of certainty, and indeed justice, require that contracts be construed in accordance with the established principles. The parties are always able by the choice of appropriate language to draft their contract so as to produce a different legal effect. The choice is theirs".

Approach of Hobhouse J is open to criticism on a number of grounds

1. Not all parties have legal advice.

2. Saying parties can contract out of a rule is not a reason for a rule to exist.

3. Parties must bear the cost of negotiating their way out of the rule.

– Notwithstanding these points - COA has endorsed the Canada Steamship rules in clear terms on a number of occasions recently *(EE Caledonia Ltd v Orbit Valve Co Europe [1994]) (The Fiona [1994])*

H of L however, took a milder approach in *HIH Casualty and General Insurance Ltd v Chase Manhattan Bank [2003]*

1. Paramount task of the court is to give effect to the intention of the parties (Lord Bingham, Lord Hoffmann, Lord Hobhouse, Lord Scott)

– Guidelines laid down by Lord Morton - are tools to be used by the courts, and they are not their masters *(Lictor Anstalt v Mir Steel UK Ltd [2012])*

1. Lordships recognised situations where the courts will more readily infer that the intention of the parties, to exclude liability for negligence of party.

This can be seen from the speech of Lord Bingham:

– "There can be no doubting the general authority of [Lord Morton's principles], which have been applied in many cases, and the approach indicated is sound. The courts should not ordinarily infer that a contracting has given up rights which the law confers upon him to an extent greater than the contract terms indicate he has chosen to do; and if the contract terms can take legal and practical effect without denying him the rights he would ordinarily enjoy if the other party is negligent, they will be read as not denying him those rights unless they are so expressed as to make clear that they do"

– Rules represent judicial hesitance and caution to conclude that one party has willingly agreed to exclude the other party from the consequences of his negligence

– Courts post-*Investors Compensation Scheme*, have shown body of their decisions suggest that the rules have little or no positive or helpful contribution to make to the resolution of the case *(National Westminster Bank v Utrecht-America Finance Company [2001])*

Fundamental Breach

– Courts have developed specific rules for circumstances in which the breach of contract by the party relying on the exclusion clause is fundamental.

2 distinct approaches

1. **Rule of law approach**

– It was not possible to exclude.

– Lord Denning – used this rule to control unreasonable exclusion clauses

1. Rule of construction approach

– Question of construction, under which the clause was interpreted against the party seeking to rely on it

Ex. Suisse Atlantique Societe d'Armament Maritime SA v NV Rotterdamsche Kolen Centrale [1967]

– H of L - held that latter approach was the correct one... but...

– Their Lordships' judgement was not clear

– Lack of clarity led to first approach being used again in *Harbutt's Plasticine Ltd v Wayne Tank Pump Co Ltd [1970]*.

– Finally, clear, in *Photo Production Ltd v Securicor Transport Ltd [1980]*, that first rule was no longer law.

Facts

– Claimant's owned a factory and contracted with the defendants

– The defendants contracted to provide periodic visits to the claimants' factory for security reasons.

– During a, an employee was cold so started a small fire to keep himself warm

– This fire then spread and burned the entire factory down.

– Claimants sought to recover damages for the fire (£648,000)

– But the defendants relied on an exclusion clause: *"under no circumstances... were they to be responsible for any injurious act or default by any employee... unless such act or default could have been foreseen and avoided by the exercise of due diligence on the part of [the defendants]"*

Judgement

– H of L – question of construction as to whether the clause covered a fundamental breach.

– On the facts, the defendants were not liable

– The exclusion cause had covered the breach.

– Confusion created by the rule of law approach

– Now, clauses interpreted on construction. More serious a breach, less likely it is to be interpreted as covering that breach.

Neil LJ (Edmund Murray Ltd v BSP International Foundations Ltd (1933)

– "It is always necessary when considering an exemption clause to decide whether as a matter of construction it extends to exclude or restrict the liability in question, but if it does, it is no longer permissible at common law to reject or circumvent the clause by treating it as inapplicable to "a fundamental breach" (Unfair Contract Terms Act 1977, s9)

Therefore if a contracting party wishes to exclude liability for...

1. Breach of a fundamental term (term which goes to the root of the contract or forms the essential character of the contract - *Karsales (Harrow) Ltd v Wallis [1956]*)

2. Refusal to perform obligations *(Sze Hai Tong Bank Ltd v Rambler Cyle Co Ltd [1959])*

3. Any breach that will have severe consequences…
… then he must use clear words to indicate this intention.

Other common law controls upon exclusion clauses

– These limits are now less significant due to the intervention of parliament

– Cannot misrepresent the effect of a clause *(Curtis v Chemical Cleaning and Dyeing Co Ltd [1951])*

– Clauses can be overridden by express statement before or at the time of contracting. *(Couchman v Hill [1947])*

– Still no power at common law to find a party cannot rely on a clause simply because it is unreasonable.

The Unfair Contract Terms Act 1977

— Parliament has taken a significant role in determining use of exclusion clauses.

— Main legislation is Unfair Contract Terms Act 1977 (UCTA) (also note, Unfair Terms in Consumer Contracts Regulations 1999)

— UCTA is complex.

— Act gives the court powers to regulate exclusion clauses significantly,

— However, there is no general doctrine of fairness or unreasonableness in English Law.

— Only some types of clauses are regulated under UCTA.

Consequence of this approach

— Parliament has to define an exclusion or a limitation clause; courts then must interpret the definition.

— Focus on the *form of the clause* which is the subject of the control, not the substance of the contract as a whole.

— All rests on whether the individual contract's clause falls into the defined clause.

— If the clause comes under the definition, it will be subjected to the reasonableness test.

— If it falls outside the Act's definition, no general doctrine of unfairness or unreasonableness to which the party seeking to set aside the term can rely on.

— Difficulties have arisen in determining the scope of the Act, with parties who seek to rely on clauses arguing they fall outside the scope of the act.

Negligence liability

Act first deals with clauses seeking to exclude liability for negligence.
Section 2

1. A person cannot by reference to any contract term or to a notice given to persons generally or to particular persons exclude or restrict his liability for death or personal injury resulting from negligence

2. In the case of other loss or damage, a person cannot so exclude or restrict his liability for negligence except in so far as the term or notice satisfies the requirement of reasonableness

3. Where a contract term or notice purports to exclude or restrict liability for negligence a person's agreement to or awareness of it is not of itself to be taken as indicating his voluntary acceptance of any risk

— **So this section only applies to "negligence",** so that it doesn't apply to attempts to exclude or restrict liability which is strict - liability which occurs irrespective of fault .

Negligence is defined in section 1(1) as:
the breach -

1. of any obligation, arising from the express or implied terms of a contract, to take reasonable care or exercise reasonable skill in the performance of the contract;

2. of any common law duty to take reasonable care or exercise reasonable skill (but not any stricter duty);

3. of the common duty of care imposed by the Occupiers' Liability Act 1957 or the Occupiers' Liability Act (Northern Ireland) 1957

— An act can be negligence even where breach of duty was intentional rather than inadvertent, or because liability for it arose vicariously rather than directly (s 1(4))

— **Secondly** - section 2 applies only clauses which try to exclude or restrict only "business liability".

Business liability is defined in section 1(3) as:

liability for breach of obligations or duties arising -

1. from things done or to be done by a person in the course of a business (whether his own business or another's) or

2. from the occupation of premises used for business purposes of the occupier...

— Business (section 14) defined as including a profession and the activities of any government department or local or public authority

— **Thirdly** - the section also applies for non-contractual notices which purport to exclude or restrict liability for negligence.

— **Fourthly** – two different methods of control exist in the section:

1. Section 2(1) - contract term or notice which seeks to exclude or restrict liability for negligence causing death or personal injury is void

— Personal injury (s14) - including "any disease and any impairment of physical or mental condition".

1. Section 2(2) – other terms which don't cover personal injury or death are valid only if they satisfy the requirement of reasonableness

Jurisdictional issues which have arisen, or may arise, under section 2

— Section limited to negligence.

— Negligence - the breach of an obligation or a duty

— Section 2 has therefore been drafted in **defensive terms;**

— There is an assumption of breach and so does not seem to extend to clauses defining the parties' obligations.

Obligations?

What happens when the clause in question simply defines the obligations of the parties and therefore fell outside the scope of section 2?

Ex. Phillips Products Ltd v Hyland and Hamstead Plant Hire Co Ltd [1987]

Facts

— Defendants hired a JCB excavator with a driver to claimant.

— **Condition 8** - driver to be regarded as the employee of the claimants

— Driver negligently crashed into claimant's factory.

— Claimants' sued, and the defendants tried to rely upon condition 8.

— Claimants argued that condition 8 was caught by section 2(2) of UCTA and that it was not reasonable.

— Defendants argued that condition 8 was not caught by section 2(2) because there had been no breach — the condition had simply defined obligations.

This argument was rejected by the COA

Judgement

— **Slade LJ** - in considering whether there has been a breach of duty under section 1(1), court should leave out defendant's account of the clause they try to rely on.
Why should this be the case?

— Slade LJ claimed to find further support for his analysis in section 13(1) of the Act which extends the scope of section 2, to encompass "terms and notices which exclude or restrict the relevant obligation or duty".

— Function of this provision is to extend the scope of section 2 to certain duty-defining clauses

— Aim of provision to prevent strong contracting parties from evading the effect of the act.

— Section 13(1) doesn't give any criteria.

Scope of section 13

Ex. Smith v Eric S Bush [1990]

- **Lord Templeman** - the act subjected to regulation "All exclusion notices which would in common law provide a defence to an action for negligence".

- **Lord Griffiths** - interpreted section 13 as "introducing" a "but for" test in relation to the notice excluding liability". That's to say a court must decide whether a duty of care would exist "but for" the exclusion clause.

- **Lord Jauncey** - the wording of section 13 was "entirely appropriate to cover a disclaimer which prevents a duty coming into existence".

Does Act catch all duty-defining clauses?

- Ridiculous conclusions if act caught all duty defining clauses.

- Confusion in the courts has caused a lack of clarity.

- Courts may be willing to depart from the "but for" test. *(Titan Steel Wheels Ltd v Royal Bank of Scotland plc [2010])*.

- However, UCTA has, at its core, a misconception of the function of exclusion clauses.

- While this remains, not difficult to see more issues arising as to which clauses fall within the scope of that act.

Examples of difficulties

1. *Ex. Thompson v T Lohan (Plant Hire) Ltd [1987]*

- This case can be contrasted with *Phillips v Hyland*

Facts

- Hiring of an employee and a JCB excavator, driver negligently causes damage.

- New version of condition 8 was included in the contract, dispute amongst parties' as to its effect.

Judgement
Held that condition 8 was not caught by section 2 of UCTA

94

- **Thompson** - the driver's negligence caused the death of Mr. Thompson

- Mr. Thompson's widow recovered damages from the general employees who then sought to recover an indemnity from the hiring employers under condition 8

- The hiring employers argued that condition 8 was caught by section 2(1) of the Act and was therefore ineffective

- Held condition 8 was not caught by section 2(1) and so was effective to transfer liability to the hiring employer

Division between these two cases is whether clause seeks to exclude liability towards the victim of the negligent act.

- **Thompson** - condition 8 did not attempt to exclude liability towards the victim of the driver's negligence (Mr. Thompson) – issue was instead about transfer of liability.

- **Phillips v Hyland** - condition 8 was relied upon in an effort to exclude liability – was therefore caught by act.

This distinction can lead to haphazard results in practice

- Suppose driver in *Phillips v Hyland*, instead of damaging claimant's wall, damaged a wall belonging to someone else, who sought and recovered damages from the general employer

- Section 2 would be irrelevant if there was no attempt to exclude a liability towards the victim of the negligence (the third party)

- Such conclusion makes it impossible for a lawyer to state in advance whether the clause will be caught by section 2 – this is because the effect depends on where damage falls.

Second issue:

1. *Ex. Scottish Special Housing Association v Wimpey Construction UK Ltd [1996]*

Facts

— Wimpey contracted to modernise houses owned by SSHA.

— While undertaking work house were damaged by fire, allegedly caused by negligence of Wimpey.

— Wimpey relied upon the terms of the contract as a defence:

— **Clause 18(2)** - Wimpey were liable for any damage to the property caused by their negligence "except for such loss or damage as is at the risk of the employer under clause 20(C)" of the contract

— **Clause 20(c)** - "the existing structures together with all contents thereof, shall be at the sole risk of the Employer as regards loss or damage by fire... and the Employer shall maintain adequate insurance against those risks".

Judgement

— **H of L** - the risk of damage to the property by fire had been allocated to SSHA including for negligence. Wimpey could exclude this liability.

Lord Keith - the essential question which clause 20(C) sought to answer was - who should insure against the contractor's negligence?
It was clearly SSHA
Questions from this case:

1. H of L didn't apply the *Canada Steamship* rules to construe this clause, despite the effect of this clause enabling Wimpey to exclude liability for their own negligence.

— Held to exclude liability for negligence, even though the word "negligence" wasn't used in the contract terms.

1. H of L didn't consider any alternative sources of liability to which the clause could apply - they simply tried to give the clause its natural interpretation.

— *Canada Steamship* rules not invoked? Why?

- Second puzzle relates to applicability of UCTA

- For procedural reasons, the Act was not in the question before the court.

Would the clause have fallen within the scope of Act?

- Clause did not seek to "exclude or restrict a liability", instead it sought to allocate risk for insurance purposes.

- However, competing arguments

- Section 13(1) extends the scope of section 2 to certain duty-defining clauses

- The effect of the clause was to enable one party to exclude liability for the consequences of its own negligence.

Courts must determine whether it is the form or the substance that they are assessing.

- If they examine its **form** – this could be said to be "insurance clause" so falls outside the Scope of the Act

- Looking at the **substance** - more likely to conclude that it falls within the Scope of the Act as the clause effectively excluded liability for negligence.

"Form or substance" debate is of great significance for the future of the Act without clear approach from court.

Ex. Johnstone v Bloomsbury HA [1992]

- **Stuart-Smith LJ** - relying in part upon the Judgement of Slade LJ *(Phillips v Hyland)*, stated that "when considering the operation of section 2 of the Act the court is concerned with the substance and not the form of the contractual provision".

Liability for breach of contract

- Act also controls clauses which try to exclude or restrict liability for breach of contract

- Section 3 crucial here.

— By virtue of section 3(1) — applies deal on the written standard terms of a business. However, the act does not provide a definition for this.

Number of questions here:

— Does the requirement that the terms be "written" mean partly oral contracts fall outside.

— When does variation render a contract no longer "standard"?

— What does "deals" mean.

— What does "other's" mean?

Courts answering:

— Meaning of the word "standard"

Judge Stannard (Chester Grosvenor Hotel Co Ltd v Alfred McAlpine Management Ltd (1991)
The question was "one of fact and degree":

— "what is required for terms to be standard is that they should be so regarded by the party which advances them as its standard terms and that it should habitually contract in those terms. If it contracts also in other terms, it must be determined in any given case, and as a matter of fact, whether this has occurred so frequently that the terms in question cannot be regarded as standard, and if on any occasion a party has substantially modified its prepared terms, it is a question of fact whether those terms have been so altered that they must be regarded as not having been employed on that occasion"

— pragmatic approach

— This will reduce the ability of parties to contract around section 3 through minor and insignificant variations of contract.

— The more negotiation, the likelier it is that a contract will not be standard for purpose of section 3. *(The Flamar Pride [1990] and The Salvage Association v CAP Financial Services Ltd [1995])*
Meaning of the word "deals"

— "makes a deal" - irrespective of any negotiations before.

- Negotiations over standard terms of business do not take the case outside the scope of section 3 (St Albans City and DC v International Computers Ltd [1996])

- **Edwards-Stuart J** - "if there is any significant difference between the terms proferred and the terms of the contract actually made, then the contract will not have been made on one party's written standard terms of business" *(Yuanda UK Co Ltd v WW Gear Construction Ltd [2010])*

- "Significant" therefore becomes important.

Meaning of the word "other's"
Ex. British Fermentation Products Ltd v Compair Reavell Ltd [1999]

- Institution of Mechanical Engineers Model Form of General Conditions of Contract used to conclude a contract.

- Defendants successfully submitted section 3 (Act) didn't apply to the exclusion clause contained in the contract

- Argued the claimants had failed to prove that these terms were *the defendants'* written standard terms of business

- Conclusion important for Model Forms of Contract – used extensively in many industries.

- Forms could be completely outside the scope of section 3

- If Judge Bowsher had adopted a more liberal approach here to the interpretation of "other's", to include Model Form contracts, it wouldn't have invalidation of exclusion clauses contained in such Forms automatically.

- Instead, they would have been subjected to the reasonableness test.

Section 3(2)(a) simple, however section 3(2)(b) is more complex and entails problems:

- As against the party who deals as consumer, the other party cannot by reference to any contract term "when himself in breach of contract, exclude or restrict any liability of his in respect of the breach except in so far as the contract term satisfies the requirement of reasonableness" (s3(2)(a))

— Business liability is the liability in question.

— Subsection is defensive because it reacts to a breach.

— This time, section 13(1) does not extend. Only applies to section 2, 6 and 7.

— Duty-defining terms can be caught by 3(2)(b) - states that the other party cannot by reference to any contract term claim to be entitled -

1. to render a contractual performance substantially different from that which was reasonably expected of him, or

2. in respect of the whole or any party of his contractual obligation, to render no performance at all,
   except in so far as... the contract term satisfies the requirement of reasonableness

— subsection applies where no breach, breach caught under 3(2)(a).

— Situation in mind? *(AXA Sun Life Services plc v Campbell Martin Ltd [2011]) – holiday company changing holiday location without breaching contract and the change is not what the other party might reasonably expect.*

— Difficult to ascertain "reasonable expectations"?

Scope of section, COA in *Timeload Ltd v British Telecommunications plc [1995]*
Facts

— Clause 18 gave BT the right "at any time" to terminate the contract by giving one months' notice.

— Claimant's sought to argue the clause was within section 3(2)(b)

— BT argued that the claimants could not reasonably expect the enjoyment of the service for an indefinite period. This was not what the contract was offering, so couldn't expect it in any reasonable sense.

Judgement

Sir Thomas Bingham MR stated:

- "if a customer reasonably expects a service to continue until BT has substantial reason to terminate it, it seems to me at least arguable that a clause purporting to authorise BT to terminate it without reason purports to permit partial or different performance from that which the customer expected".

- Even when case didn't meet precise terms of section 3(2)(b) - the subsection could be used by courts as a "platform for invalidating or restricting the operation of an oppressive clause in a situation of the present, very special, kind".

- Can question this extremely wide interpretation of section 3(2)(b)

- If the courts don't place importance on the terms of the contract in finding the expectations of the parties, then it appears to be impossible to limit the subsection. Very wide.

Employment Appeal Tribunal in *Peninsula Business Services Ltd v Sweeney [2004]* – more narrow approach:

Facts

- Employment contract term: "an employee has no claim whatsoever to any commission payments that would otherwise have been generated and paid if he is not in employment on the date when they would normally have been paid".

- The claimant resigned meaning he surrendered substantial commission payments – he could have claimed it had he stayed in employment.

- Claimant questioned whether the defendants could not give him the commission because the clause seemed to allow the defendants to change contractual obligations so they were significantly different from what the defendant reasonably expected.

Judgement

- EAT: the defendants were simply operating the contract in accordance with its terms, rejected idea of differing from reasonable expectation.

- **Rimer J** - the clause "simply defined the limits' of the claimant's rights and did not purport to "cut down or restrict his rights in any way".

- Open to criticism...

- The aim of section 3(2)(b) was to extend the scope of the Act to certain contract terms which define the rights of the parties. Therefore, this judgment can be seen as neglecting this aim.

- Just because the clause defined rights shouldn't have taken the term outside the scope of the subsection.

- Distinction between this case and *Timeload* rests on significance court placed on terms relied on.

- Approach of the EAT in *Peninsula,* is the preferred one. The court ought to attach considerable importance to the terms of the contract when ascertaining the reasonable expectations of the parties.

- Unless it can be shown that the party relying on the term of the contract, either knew or ought to have known, that the other party to the contract was not aware of the term in the contract and could not reasonably be expected to know of it.

- The Act also regulates other clauses which try to exclude or restrict liability for breach of contract.

- In contracts for the sale or hire-purchase of goods, implied terms as to title cannot be excluded or restricted through a term in the contract (s 6(1));

- A sellers implied undertaking for descriptions, quality and fitness can't be excluded through reference to contract terms.

Two further points should be noted

1. Not just business liability in question here.

- However, questions as to quality and fitness for purpose only really apply in the context of business.

1. Courts must look at specific matters in considering whether such a term is reasonable (s 11(3))

- For contracts of hire or exchange, any term which purports to exclude or restrict liability for breach of an obligation due to extent to which goods' corresponded with their description or sample or their quality and fitness for any particular purpose is void as against a consumer (s 7(2)) and, as against anyone else, must satisfy the reasonableness test (s 7(3))

- Liability for breach of the obligations contained in **section 2 of the Supply of Goods and Services Act 1982** - cannot be excluded or restricted

Attempts at evasion

- The Act contains provisions designed to combat an attempt to evade the sections.

Section 13(1) states:

- To the extent that this Part of this Act prevents the exclusion or restriction of any liability it also prevents -

1. making the liability or its enforcement subject to restrictive or onerous conditions;

2. excluding or restricting any right or remedy in respect of the liability, or subjecting a person to any prejudice in consequence of his pursuing any such right or remedy;

3. excluding or restricting rules of evidence or procedure;

- and sections 2,5,6,7 also prevent excluding or restricting liability by reference to terms and notices which exclude or restrict the relevant obligation or duty

- Section has no independent effect: it extends the scope of sections 2 and 5 to 7

- Sections 2, 5,6 and 7 all deal with whether terms are void, or valid, etc. The court must always to refer to whichever of these sections is applicable when applying the reasonableness test.

Extensions can both be criticised and shown to offer some useful effects:
Example

– Trying to exclude a right of set-off falls within its scope *(Steward Gill Ltd v Horatio Myer & Co Ltd [1992])*

Section 10:

– A restrictive or exclusionary term, contained in a separate contract rather than the liability inducing contract, is ineffective in so far as it attempts to take away a right to enforce a liability which under the Act cannot be excluded or restricted.

– This section tries to prevent secondary contracts being used to evade the act.

The reasonableness test:

– This test is central to the operation of the Act.

– **Section 11(1) provides that:**

– "in relation to a contract term, the requirement of reasonableness... is that the term shall have been a fair and reasonable one to be included having regard to the circumstances which were, or ought reasonably to have been known to or in the contemplation of the parties when the contract was made".

– Breach assessed at the time of the contract formation.

– Party trying to rely on the exclusion clause must show it is reasonable (s11(5))

Factors in assessing reasonableness:

1. Bargaining power of the parties

2. Negotiation of clause

3. Legal advice relied on by parties

4. Insurance availability

5. Extent to which the party seeking to rely on the exclusion clause sought to explain its effect when contracting.

Phillips v Hyland – demonstration of reasonableness:

– Held that condition 8 - failed the reasonableness test:

– Why? Claimants did not generally hire JCB excavators and their drivers – little knowledge, no time for insurance, no choice as to the driver provided.

– Instead, the defendants were in best position to take out insurance and bear the loss

– These factors combined, suggested that condition 8 was not reasonable

– No single approach and intervention has varied.

– However, Appellate courts should treat the trial Judge's finding on the issue of reasonableness with the utmost respect unless the decision was "erroneous in principle or was plainly and obviously wrong" *(George Mitchell (Chesterhall) Ltd v Finney Lock Seeds Ltd [1983])(Cleaver v Schyde Investments Ltd [2011])*

– Certainty sacrificed here.

A lot determined by the facts of the individual case…
But a number propositions about test can be stated with a degree of certainty:

1. **The court must work out meaning of clause prior to determining if it passes the reasonableness test** *(Watford Electronics Ltd v Sanderson CFL Ltd [2001])*

– Wide interpretation may lead to conclusion clause is unreasonable.

– Conversely, a narrow interpretation more likely to be reasonable *(Regus (UK) Ltd v Epcot Solutions Ltd [2008])*

1. **Clause as a whole is assessed:**

– Not limited to section of clause that is being relied on *(Stewart Gill Ltd v Horatio Myer & Co Ltd [1992])*

– This proposition flows from the fact that **Section 11(1) states that:**

– The time for assessing the reasonableness of the clause is the time at which the contract was made (at which point it will not be known which part of it will be relied upon by the defendant) and not the time of the breach

— The court "should not be too ready to focus on remote possibilities or to accept arguments that a clause fails the test by reference to relatively uncommon or unlikely situations" *(FG Wilson (Engineering) Ltd v John Holt & Co (Engineering) Ltd [2012])*

— Focus should be on events that would have been considered by parties as being "realistic and not unlikely" at the time of agreement.

1. **The court cannot remove unreasonable aspects of a clause leaving reasonable section intact:** *(Stewart Gill Ltd v Horatio Myer & Co Ltd [1992])*

— Important for drafting.

— Not advisable to rely on a broad, all-encompassing clause, if only one part of it is held unreasonable the rest will also be treated like this.

— But courts may be able to break down a clause if it can operate as such- at least where the different parts of the clause are held to be "independent" of each other (Regus (UK) Ltd v Epcot Solutions Ltd) or "the different parts are performing different functions" (Murphy & Sons Ltd v Johnston Precast Ltd [2008])

1. **Equality of bargaining power**

— The greater the inequality of the bargaining power of the parties, the less likely it is that the clause will pass the reasonableness test

Ex. Chadwick LJ (Watford Electronics Ltd v Sanderson CFL Ltd)

— "Where experienced businessmen representing substantial companies of equal bargaining power negotiate an agreement, they may be taken to have had regard to the matters known to them. They should, in my view be taken to be the best judge of the commercial fairness of the agreement which they have made; including the fairness of each of the terms in that agreement. They should be taken to be the best judge on the question whether the terms of the agreement are reasonable. The court should not assume that either is likely to commit his company to an agreement which he thinks is unfair, or which he thinks includes unreasonable terms. Unless satisfied that one party has, in effect, taken unfair advantage of the other - or that a term is so unreasonable that it cannot properly have been understood or considered - the court should not interfere".

— More restrained judgments in... *(Britvic Soft Drinks Ltd v Messer UK Ltd [2002])*

— Some reluctance to strike down a term which has been freely agreed between large commercial parties – seen as best position to work out interests. *(Granville Oil & Chemicals v Davis Turner [2003])*

1. **The insurance consequences are relevant in court**

— Availability of insurance the dominant factor, not the actual insurance positons of the parties. *(The Flamar Pride [1990])*

— Therefore just because defendant has decided to insure themselves for a sum greater than the limitation clause in the contract, this does not mean that the limitation clause is unreasonable *(Moores v Yakely Associates Ltd [1999])*

1. **Widely drafted exclusion clauses are not advisable**

— Courts are likely to look unfavourably upon exclusion clauses drafted to undermine express promises. *(Lease Management Services Ltd v Purnell Secretarial Services Ltd [1994])*

1. **Enforcement not crucial**

— Just because a defendant has not always enforced the clause, does not show the clause to be inevitably unreasonable.

Ex. Schenkers Ltd v Overland Shoes Ltd [1998]

— COA - in finding a clause to be reasonable, found it relevant that the clause was in common use.

— inequality of bargaining power between the parties was also not apparent.

— In that context, the fact the clause was not enforced in practice didn't mean it couldn't be relied on.

1. **It is not advisable to include two very different types of loss within the same limitation clause**

Ex. Overseas Medical Supplies Ltd v Orient Transport Services Ltd [1999]
Facts

— The defendant freight-forwarders failed to insure the claimants' goods; they were required to insure under the contract.

— The defendants had limited liability to £600

Judgement

— Held that, limitation of £600 was reasonable for claim of direct loss (e.g., caused by the default of the defendants when transporting the goods), however, it could not also cover the failure to insure – this was not reasonable.

Reason for this conclusion related to different consequences of breach.

— By trying to include two very distinct and different losses within the same clause, the defendants made it impossible to demonstrate such a clause could be reasonable.

1. **Limitation more likely to be found reasonable than a total exclusion.**

— No guarantee, but likelihood increases.

Ex. St Albans City and District CC v International Computers Ltd [1996]

— A clause in a computer contract which limited liability to £100,000 was found to have be unreasonable

— The trial judge (whose judgement was upheld by COA) found an important factor to be the unequal bargaining power

— There was also no justification of the clause.

– Seems where a limitation clause is used, party should attempt to provide some objective justification for the selection of that figure.

– Simple picking a figure will increase likelihood of finding that the clause is unreasonable *(The Salvage Association v CAP Financial Services Ltd [1995])*

Excepted Contracts

– Act doesn't apply to agreements such as contracts of insurance and contracts which concern the transfer of an interest in land

Section 26:

– the limits imposed by the Act on the extent to a party can exclude or restrict liability through using a contract term don't apply to liability arising under an international supply contract, nor are the terms of such a contract subject to the reasonableness requirement under section 3 or 4

Sections 26 (3)(4):

– **International supply contract** - a contract for the sale of goods or one under or in pursuance of which the possession or ownership of goods passes and which is made by parties whose places of business (or habitual residences) are in the territories of different States

One of the further condition:

1. the goods in question are, at the time of the conclusion of the contract, in the course of carriage, or will be carried from the territory of one State to the territory of another, or

2. the acts constituting the offer and acceptance have been done in the territories of different states, or

3. the contract provides for the goods to be delivered to the territory of a State other than the State within whose territory the acts constituting the offer and acceptance were done

Section 26(4)(a):

— Does not require a seller or hirer to have undertaken an obligation to deliver the contractual goods to another state; it suffices that, at the time of the conclusion of agreement, the goods will be carried from the territory of one state to the territory of another *(Trident Turboprop (Dublin) Ltd v First Flight Couriers Ltd [2009])*

— Reference to "the acts constituting the offer and acceptance" (section 26 (4)(b)), is a reference to the "totality of the acts which constitute the offer and acceptance, including the making and receiving of each" *(Air Transworld Ltd v Bombardier Inc [2012])*

— But in the case of section 26(4)(c) - it's not sufficient to prove that the goods have been delivered "in" the territory of a state other than the State within whose territory the acts constituting the offer and acceptance were done

— Goods must be delivered "to" that country; in other words, the goods must have been delivered from a country which was outside that territory *(Amiri Flight Authority v BAE Systems plc [2003])*

— Phrase "made by the parties" (section 26(3)) refers to the principals to the contract in question and not to the agents *(Ocean Chemical Transport Inc v Exnor Craggs Ltd [2000])*

Section 29(1):

— The Act does not regulate any contractual provision which is authorised or required by the express terms or by necessary implication of an enactment, or any contractual term which is necessary in order to secure compliance with an international agreement to which the UK is a party.

Section 27(1):

— where the law applicable to a contract is the law of any part of the UK only by choice of the parties, sections 2 to 7 of the Act do not operate as part of the law applicable to the contract

— Foreign parties who choose English law as the law applicable to the contract do not thereby subject themselves to sections 2

110

to 7 of UCTA (but rules which regulate attempts to exclude liability for misrepresentation are applicable to such contracts)

– Limits found in section 27(2)

Section 27(2):

– the controls contained in the Act cannot be evaded by the choice of a law outside the UK as the governing law if it appears that the choice of law was imposed wholly or mainly to enable the party imposing it to evade the operation of the Act or where one of the parties dealt as a consumer, was then habitually resident in the UK and the essential steps for the making of the contract were taken in the UK

Conclusion

– UCTA (1977) major attempt to control exclusion clauses.

– Not wholly satisfactory.

– Biggest problem is in working out the function of clauses: does it define the nature and extent of obligations or is it a defence to a breach of contract?

– The courts have traditionally seen exclusion clauses in defensive terms and although UCTA is cast in defensive terms.

– But if it is conceded that the Act does apply to duty-defining clauses, how can it be ascertained which duty-defining terms are caught by the Act?

– Only solution lies in treating exclusion clause like any other term of the contract and only intervening to control them where they are shown to be "unfair" or "unconscionable".

– 2005 - Law Commission and Scottish Law Commission recommended the introduction of legislation that would unify UCTA and Unfair Terms in Consumer Contracts Regulations

– In other respects, Law Commission proposed to leave UCTA largely unchanged (in terms of substance rather than drafting style)

— They recommended the redrafting of section 3 - but its substance would be kept

— Report represented careful attempt to clarify and to simplify the law

— But it hasn't been implemented

7. Misrepresentation

What is a misrepresentation?

1. Unambiguous false statement of fact or law

2. Directed to the party who is misled.

3. Must induce entrance to the contract.

The sections in more detail:

A statement of existing fact or law

— Traditionally rule required *unambiguous false statement of existing fact*

— Now, statement of law encompassed into actionable misrepresentation

— Case for this change.

Ex. Kleinwort Benson Ltd v Lincoln City Council [1999]

— H of L - money paid under a mistake of law can be recovered as if paid under a mistake of fact (Ex. *Brennan v Bolt Burden (a firm) [2004]*)

— misrepresentation of law can bring about a cause of action *(Pankhania v London Borough of Hackney [2002])*

— Need for a statement — mere failure to disclose therefore can't be a representation.

— Flexible, wide approach for identifying a "statement", a statement can be made by conduct.

— The statement must relate to an *existing fact*

3 categories have been held not to constitute statements of existing fact

1. **"Mere puff"**

– So vague it is neither a term nor a statement of fact.

Ex. Dimmock v Hallett (1866)

– Turner LJ - a representation that land was "fertile and improvable" too vague.

– But the more specific the statement, less likely to be viewed by the courts as a mere puff. *(Carlill v Carbolic Smoke Ball Co [1893])*

1. **A statement of opinion or belief which proves to be unfounded is not a false statement of fact**

Ex. Bisset v Wilkinson [1927]
Facts

– A vendor of a farm in NZ, represented to a prospective purchaser that the land could carry 2000 sheep – farm had not had sheep on it before.

– In reality, it couldn't carry the sheep. Purchaser tried to set aside the contract on the ground of the vendor's misrepresentation

Judgement
Statement was an honestly held opinion.
Bisset was **distinguished** in the case of...
Esso Petroleum Ltd v Mardon [1976]
Facts

– Esso represented to the defendant, a potential tenant that a petrol station was under construction.

– Statement that station likely to reach 200,000 gallons per year

– But the local authority blocked location.

– The station had to be built back to front.

– Esso assured the defendant wouldn't affect anything.

– Throughput only 78,000 gallons per year

– Defendant incurred considerable losses. Debt to Esso.

- Esso sought to repossess the station.

- Defendant counterclaimed for damages for breach of contract and for negligent misrepresentation

Judgement

- COA - the statement was actionable

- Lord Denning distinguished *Bisset* because - "the land had never been used as a sheep farm and both parties were equally able to form an opinion as to its carrying capacity".

- Esso, on the other hand, had special knowledge and skill in the forecasting of the throughput of petrol. Forecasts held to be made with "reasonable care and skill".

- Held Esso did not exercise reasonable care and skill and were therefore liable to the defendant in damages

Ex. Bowen LJ - Smith v Land and House Property Corp (1884)
Bowen LJ

- "the facts are equally known to both parties, what one says to the other is frequently nothing but an expression of opinion... But if the facts are not equally well known to both sides, then a statement of opinion by one who knows the facts best involves very often a statement of material fact, for he impliedly states that he knows facts which justify his opinion".

When the principles established in Esso and Smith are combined, it can be deduced that:

- "Where the representor has greater knowledge than the representee, the courts will imply that the representation must be made with reasonable care and skill *(Esso)* and that the representor knows facts which justify his opinion *(Smith)*"

1. **A statement of intention is not a statement of fact/nor is a promise a statement of fact**

- A person who doesn't carry out their stated intention does not thereby make a misrepresentation *(Wales v Wadham [1977])*

– But a person who misrepresents his present intention does make a false statement of fact.

Ex. *Edgington v Fitzmaurice (1885)*

Facts

– Company directors invited the public to subscribe for debentures; this was done on the basis that any funds raised would be used to grow and expand the company.

– Really just wanted to pay off debt.

Judgement

– Actual intention at the time of statement was misrepresented.

Addressed to the party misled

Must be able to demonstrate representation was addressed to the party misled
2 ways in which a representation may be addressed to the party misled

1. Direct communication
2. Addressed to a third party with the intention it be passed on to the claimant.

Ex. *Commercial Banking Co of Sydney v RH Brown and Co [1972]*

Facts

– Defendant bank misrepresented to the claimants' bank the financial standing of one of the claimants' customers

– The claimants' bank passed this on, and the claimant suffered losses as a result.

Judgement

– Defendants were liable to the claimants because they knew misrepresentation to the bank would be communicated to claimant.

Inducement

Representation must be an inducement to enter into the contract, and possibly it must also be a material misrepresentation

- — materiality requirement controversial.

- — In old cases, misrepresentation must be material *(Mathias v Yetts (1882))*

- — *Meaning of* **materiality** - misrepresentation must have been such as would affect the judgement of a reasonable man who was making decision as to contracting.

- — But requirement is doubted.

- — Modern courts done tend to look for distinction between inducement and materiality.

- — Rather... an inference of inducement is often found as a result of finding of materiality, so that materiality becomes a part of the inquiry into whether or not the misrepresentation induced the contract.

Orthodox position today:

- — If the misrepresentation **would have** induced a reasonable person to enter into the contract, then presumption created that it did induce the representee to enter into the contract. The onus of proof then moves to the representor to show that the representee did not actually rely on the representation *(Museprime Properties Ltd v Adhill Properties Ltd (1991))*

On the other hand...

- — Where the misrepresentation **would not have** induced a reasonable person to enter into the contract, onus is moved to the representee to show that the misrepresentation did induce him to enter into the contract (Dadourin Group International Inc v Simms [2009])

Difficult case when an innocent and immaterial misrepresentation induces a representee to enter into a contract

- Extremely unlikely that a representee would be able to prove that he was induced to contract by an immaterial misrepresentation

- However, there remains a possibility this could happen; this suggests courts should operate with caution before abandoning the materiality requirement.

- Fraud is an exception — cannot say immaterial. *(Ross River Ltd v Cambridge City Football Club Ltd [2007])*

Regardless of the materiality requirement, there is no doubt that representation must induce the contract... it must induce the actual claimant to enter into the contract
Ex. Edgington v Fitzmaurice (1885)

- Misrepresentation doesn't have to be the sole inducement, nor must it have been "decisive".

Ex. Raiffeisen Zentralbank Osterreich AG v Royal Bank of Scotland plc [2010]

- However, it is not sufficient for the claimant to show that "he was supported or encouraged in reaching his decision by the representation in question".

- Claimant must be able to provide that the representation played a **"real and substantial"** part in inducing him to contract.

Ex. JEB Fasteners v Marks, Bloom and Co [1983]
"Real and substantial" requirement was not found in this case
Facts

- Defendants negligently prepared the accounts for a company the claimants wished to buy.

- The claimants had had reservations about the accounts when they received them; they still decided to take over — fuelled by a desire to acquire the services of two of the directors.

- Take-over failed commercially, and claimants sued defendants.

Judgement

118

— COA - dismissed action. The defendants' representation did not play a *"real and substantial"* part in inducing the claimants to act

— To prove that a representation played a *"real and substantial"* part, the claimants must prove that *"but for such representation"* he *"would not have entered into the contract on the terms on which he did, even though there were other matters but for which he would not have done so either"*

— a court will ask what the claimant would have done if no representation had been made to him.

3 situations in which a claimant will be unable to show that the representation induced the contract

1. **claimant was unaware of the representation (Horsfall v Thomas (1862))**

2. **The claimant was aware that the representation was not true**

3. **The claimant did not allow the representation to affect his judgement**

— No effect if claimant views representation as being unimportant *(Smith v Chadwick (1884))* or where he relies upon his own judgement

This rule does not apply to the claimant who has the opportunity to discover the truth himself but does not take it

— Here, claimants remain entitled to relief against the misrepresentor *(Redgrave v Hurd (1881))* (although in light of the decision of the H of L in Smith *v Eric S Bush [1990]*),

— BUT - *Redgrave* may not apply where it was reasonable to expect the representee to make use of the opportunity, yet in fact, failed to do so.

Similar rule applies in the case where the representor "corrects" his misrepresentation prior to reliance

– In such a case the representor must demonstrate their correction was actually brought to the representee.

The types of misrepresentation

All types of misrepresentation entitle the representee to rescind the contract but not all types of misrepresentation give rise to an action for damages

Fraudulent misrepresentation

– Contract may be set aside, tort of deceit

– Meaning in the law is narrow

Ex. Lord Herschell - Derry v Peek (1889)
3 Propositions were established

1. There must be proof of fraud

2. Fraud is proved when it is demonstrated that a false representation has been made, knowingly, without belief in its truth, or recklessly, careless whether it be true or false

– Unreasonableness of belief does not of itself constitute fraud; it simply provides evidence of dishonesty on the part of the maker of the statement *(Angus v Clifford [1891])*

1. If fraud is proved, the motive of the person guilty of it is not relevant.

Ex. Polhill v Walter (1832)
Facts

– Representor knew that his statement was false, but his motive in making the statement was to benefit his principal and not to benefit himself, no intention to injure anyone else either.

Judgement

– Liable in the tort of deceit

Negligent misrepresentation at common law

- Post *Derry v Peek,* assumed that negligent misrepresentation was not actionable in tort because liability in tort arose only in cases of fraudulent misrepresentation *(Le Lievre v Gould [1893])*

Rejected by H of L in...
Ex. Nocton v Lord Ashburton [1914]

- H of L accepted that negligent misrepresentation could be actionable, only actionable if there was a pre-existing contractual relationship between the parties or a "fiduciary relationship" existed.

- Restrictive, narrow approach prevailed in England as late as 1951 (Candler v Crane, Christmas and Co [1951])

In 1964 however, the H of L expanded the ambit of liability for negligent misrepresentation
Ex. Hedley Byrne v Heller [1964]
Facts

- Claimants were advertising agents who booked advertising space on behalf of their clients, *Easipower Ltd,* and they were personally liable if Easipower defaulted

- Claimants sought from the defendants (Easipower's bankers), a reference for the financial soundness of Easipower

- Defendants replied – Easipower were "considered good for its ordinary business transactions".

- The claimants relied on this and placed orders which resulted in a loss to them of £17,000

- Claimants alleged that the defendants were negligent in the preparation of the reference.

Judgement

- Reference provided with "without responsibility" so failed in claim.

- But the H of L would have allowed the claim to succeed *had it not been for the disclaimer*

– In so concluding, the scope of liability in tort for negligent misrepresentation significantly widened

But now the **limits** *of Hedley Byrne must be considered.*
Approaches

1. **Utilise the concept of a "special relationship" between the claimant and defendant**

– Content of this "special relationship" is controversial.

– Elements seemed to be *voluntary assumption of responsibility by the defendant* and *foreseeable detrimental reliance by the claimant.*

– The courts then distanced themselves from the voluntary assumption of responsibility test *(Caparo Industries plc v Dickman[1990])*... instead relying on a number of factors in deciding whether or not to impose liability *(Neil LJ - James McNaughten Papers Group plc v Hicks Anderson & Co (a firm) [1991])*

– However, assumption of responsibility test is back in favour now *(Lord Goff - Spring v Guardian Assurance plc [1995]* and *Lord Steyn - Williams v Natural Life Health Foods Ltd [1998])*

– The word "voluntary" has been removed – objectivity.

Lord Mustill (White v Jones [1995])

– Detected the themes of mutuality, special relationship, reliance and undertaking of responsibility, in *Hedley Byrne*

– According to Lord Mustill, *Hedley Byrne* liability arose "internally from the relationship in which the parties had together chosen to place themselves'.

Factors the court have considered to define the scope of Hedley Byrne

1. **Knowledge of the representor**

– Greater the knowledge which the representor, the more likely it is that the representor will be liable to the representee.

– **special skill?**

Ex. Mutual Life and Citizens Assurance Co v Evatt [1971]
Facts

- Majority of the Pricy Council held this element requires that the representor be in the business of giving advice for the relevant subject.

- Defendant insurance company gave claimant gratuitous advice about an investment into the defendant's sister company.
Judgement

- not liable because they were not especially skilled as investment advisers

- BUT…minority (Lord Reid and Lord Morris): a duty of care is owed by anyone who takes it upon himself to make representations, knowing that the other will justifiably rely upon his misrepresentations

Support of this view:

- Ormerod LJ - *Esso Petroleum v Mardon [1976]*

- Shaw LJ & Lord Denning - *Howard Marine and Dredging Cov A Ogden and Sons [1978]*

- On the bases of these *dicta*, *seems* minority view will be preferred

1. The purpose for which the statement is made

- If intention of representor is that the representee rely upon it, it becomes more likely the representor will be liable. *(Smith v Eric S Bush)*

- If statement is to general public, then it is unlikely that liability will be imposed *(Caparo v Dickman)*

1. It must be reasonable for the representee to rely upon the representor's statement

- Social occasions will not generally give rise to statements treated as representations. This is due to reasonableness of reliance. (Chaudhry v Prabhakar [1989])

Negligent misrepresentation at common law must be **distinguished** from any liability arising out of **section 2(1) of the Misrepresentation Act 1967**

— This is the third type of misrepresentation

Section 2(1)

- "Where a person has entered into a contract after a misrepresentation has been made to him by another party thereto and as a result thereof he has suffered loss then, if the person making the misrepresentation would be liable to damages in respect thereof had the misrepresentation been made fraudulently, that person shall be so liable notwithstanding that the misrepresentation was not made fraudulently, unless he proves that he had reasonable grounds to believe and did believe up to the time that the contract was made that the facts represented were true"

- Section 2 (1) – not guided by Hedley principle.

- Unusual terms, it imposes liability by referencing fraudulent misrepresentation (even though the misrepresentor has not been fraudulent)

Taken away from its convoluted drafting, the section states that:

- "Where a misrepresentation has been made by one contracting party to another, the party making the misrepresentation is liable to the other in damages unless he can prove that he had reasonable grounds to believe and did believe up to the time that the contract was made that his statement was true".

- The section focussed on the liability of the "other party" to the contract and not with the liability of an agent of that party *(Resolute Maritime Inc v Nippon Kaiji Kyokai, The Skopas [1983])*

The statutory right has 3 advantages over a common law negligence claim

1. **No need for Hedley Byrne relationship between the parties**

Ex. Gosling v Anderson [1972]
Facts

— Defendant was in process of selling a flat, represented to the claimant, through an estate agent, that planning permission had been obtained in relation to the building of a new garage by the house. This was not true; permission had not yet been granted.
Judgement

— COA - Roskill LJ stated that pre-1967, the claimant's action would have failed unless they could show fraud.

— Could now rely on **Section 2(1) of the 1967 Act** and was entitled to damages for the misrepresentation

1. **The representor is liable unless he proves that he had reasonable grounds to believe and did believe up to the time that the contract was made, that the facts represented were true**

— In common law, representee must demonstrate that the representor was negligent

— Belief of the representor relevant for this purpose, not any agent.

— Will not be sufficient for a representor to show an agent had reasonable grounds to believe and did believe that the representation was true

— This subsection is aimed at dealing with the liability of the "other party" to the contract, therefore only the belief of a party who can be identified with the company itself that is relevant *(MCI WorldCom International Inc v Primus Telecommunications Inc [2003])*

Difficult for a representor to discharge the onus proof under section 2(1)
Ex. Howard Marine v Ogden
Facts

— Defendants wanted to hire barges from claimants

— In negotiations, the claimants' manager represented that the deadweight capacity of each barrage was 1600 tonnes,

— Reality – only 1055 tonnes

— The defendants used the barges for six months with some difficulty.

— When they found out true capacity, they decided to stop paying for the hire.

— Claimants sued for hire charges and defendants counter-claimed, inter alia, for damages under Section 2(1) of the 1967 Act

— Representation of the claimants' manager as to the deadweight capacity of the barges was based upon his recollection of the figures in Lloyd's register – authority in shipping.

— The managers recollection was right; it was Lloyd's that was wrong

Judgement

— COA - the claimants had not discharged the burden of proof upon them.

— Hadn't demonstrated reasonable grounds to believe the statement was true

— The accurate figures could be found in the ships' documents. Claimants had failed to show any "objectively reasonable ground" for preferring the figure in Lloyd's Register.

— Burden upon the representor is a heavy one, and it is likely to enable a representee to recover, where at common law he would have failed *(Howard Marine v Ogden)*

1. **The measure of damages recoverable under section 2(1) is the measure of damages for the tort of deceit**

Ex. Royscot Trust Ltd v Rogerson [1991]
Facts

- Claimant finance company entered a hire-purchase deal with Mr. Rogerson due to a misrepresentation by the defendant car dealers

- Claimants' policy not to enter into a hire-purchase transaction unless 20% of the purchase price of a car was paid to the dealer by the customer. Defendant's aware of this.

- Mr. Rogerson agreed with the defendants to place deposit of £1200, the price of car was £7600

- Deposit was only 16% of the purchase price

- So defendants falsely stated that the price of the car was £8000 and that Mr. Rogerson had paid a deposit of £1600; producing the required 20% deposit (the case continued on assumption of no fraud).

- Claimants, on this basis, agreed to enter into a transaction.

- Mr. Rogerson then sold the car and ceased to pay the hire-purchase instalments.

Judgement

- COA - held that damages for **section 2(1)**, assessed as if there was fraud.

- The claimants were entitled to recover their actual loss directly flowing from the misrepresentation, whether or not that loss was reasonably foreseeable

The **remoteness rule** applicable, was derived from the **tort of deceit**, not the tort of negligence

- Mr. Rogerson dishonestly selling the car was a direct result of the defendants' misrepresentation.

- No break in chain of causation

- Claimants could recover damages of £3625 (difference between the £6400 advanced to Mr. Rogerson and the instalments of £2775 they received from him before his default)

Section 2(1) or tort of deceit

– Sometimes better to bring claim in tort of deceit.

– *Royscot* - reduces the practical significance of the tort of deceit

– Royscot - there is no justification for treating an innocent party as if he had been fraudulent?

Ex. Smith New Court Securities Ltd v Scrimgeour Vickers (Asset Management) Ltd [1997]

– Lord Steyn and Lord Browne-Wilkinson - Royscot had been subject to "trenchant academic criticism". "no concluded view" on whether it was correct.

– Suggestion of legislation to remedy decision.

Rules applicable to the assessment of damages should be derived from the tort of negligence, not deceit *(Gran Gelato Ltd v Richcliff (Group) Ltd [1992])*
Despite the advantages of Section 2(1), certain situations still remain in which a claimant must have recourse to a common law claim

1. **The representation made by a third party**

2. **The contract between the parties is void ab initio (e.g., on the ground of non est factum)**

– In such a case, there is no contract to which Section 2(1) can apply

1. **A court may hesitate to find the existence of a misrepresentation in a case brought under section 2(1)**

– Avon Insurance plc v Swire Fraser Ltd [2000]) and Raiffeisen Zentralbank Osterreich AG v Royal Bank of Scotland plc [2010])

1. **Section 2(1) cannot be applied to a case in which the misrepresentation is to be found in the contract itself but was not made before the contract was entered into**

– *(Leofelis SA v Lonsdale Sports Ltd [2008])*

Innocent misrepresentation

- If misrepresentation is found to be neither fraudulent nor negligent

Remedies
2 main remedies

1. **Rescission for misinterpretation**

This means setting aside the contract both retrospectively and prospectively.
DEBATE: Is this a contractual remedy?

- **Contractual remedy** – allows party to escape obligations under the contract.

- **Restitutionary remedy** – recovery of the value of the enrichment.

- Claimant might have wanted damages.

- No claim for damages in contract if contract has been set aside.

- Tort the route needed.

Rescission

Rescission for breach

- Parties escape future obligations.

Rescission for misrepresentation

- Rescission is not immediate.

- Contract is instead voidable – this gives a choice to the representee.

Rescind the contract
Need to give notice if decision is to rescind:

1. Trying to obtain declaration contract not valid.

2. Restoration of anything obtained through the contract

3. Using misrepresentation as a defence (*Redgrave v Hurd (1881)*)

Ex. Islington LBC v UCKAC [2006]

- Dyson LJ - a voidable contract continues to exist "until and unless it is set aside by an order of rescission made by the court at the instance of a party seeking to terminate it or bring it to an end".

- Odd to rest the rescission on a court, not the parties.

Limits

Right to rescind **lost** if

1. There is an **affirmation** by claimant.

2. **By the intervention of third party rights acting in good faith.**

3. **There is a lapse of time** (*Leaf v International Galleries [1950]*)

4. **It is impossible to restore the parties to pre-contract status:**

- Aim is to ensure the claimant does not benefit unfairly from their rescission. (*McKenzie v Royal Bank of Canada [1934]*)

Rescission sets aside contract for all purposes:
No contractual damages…
But… **Rescission can create personal restitutionary claim**
Ex. Whittington v Seale-Hayne (1900)
Facts

- Claimants obtained a lease of premises to breed poultry.

- Representation that premises were clean.

- Under the lease, claimants agreed to meet obligations that came with the property.

- Property in state of despair.

- Contamination, causing losses.

— Local authority ordered claimants to clean drains and carry out repairs.

Judgement

— The claimants entitled to be repaid for cost of carrying out the repairs.

— The cost was incurred due to the contract alone — obligation to repair.

— Defendant benefited from this.

— Claimants could not recover other losses — no benefit to defendant.

— Tort action needed.

Damages

— Damages may be recoverable in tort if misrepresentation was made fraudulently or negligently

Section 2(1) and 2(2) of the Misrepresentation Act 1967

— If there is no element of double recovery, a claimant may rescind and claim damages, taking asides 2(2).

Different types of misrepresentation:

1. **Fraudulent misrepresentation**

— Tort of deceit

— Protection of reliance interest

— Defendant liable for losses resulting from fraudulent inducement (remoteness included in this) *(Doyle v Olby [1969]) and (Smith New Court Securities Ltd v Scrimgeour Vickers (Asset Management) Ltd [1997])*

— **Punitive damages** - *(Kuddus v Chief Constable of Leicestershire Constabulary [2001])*

— **Aggravated damages** *(Archer v Brown [1985])*

131

1. **Negligent misrepresentation at common law**

– Tort action.

– Restore to position pre-tort.

– Losses which are a reasonably foreseeable *(The Wagon Mound (No. 1) [1961])*

– Where the representee has also been at fault, relevance of *contributory negligence (Law Reform (Contributory Negligence) Act 1945, s 1; Gran Gelato Ltd Richcliff (Group) Ltd [1992])*

Claim under section 2(1) of the Misrepresentation Act 1967
measure of damages recoverable is debatable point:

1. Damages should place claimant in position they would have found themselves in, had the misrepresentation not happened. (**reliance interest**)

2. Damages should seek to position the claimant as if the representation had been true (**expectation interest**)

Ex. Gosling v Anderson [1972] and Jarvis v Swan's Tours [1973]

– Lord Denning and Graham J *(Watts v Spence [1976])* - *expectation measure*

– Rejected: *(Royscot Trust Ltd v Rogerson [1991])* and *(Sharneyford Supplies Ltd v Barrington Black and Co [1987])* – RELIANCE

Why did reliance win?
Rests on distinction between a promise and a representation:

– A representor asserts the truth of what they say and allows, encourages or invites *reliance* on what has been said.

– They do not promise anything.

– damages assessed by treating representor as if they were fraudulent *(Royscot Trust Ltd v Rogerson)*

– This means remoteness rules applicable for tort of deceit; not the tort of negligence

- Contributory negligence can affect damages under Section 2(1) *(Gran Gelato Ltd v Richcliff (Group) Ltd)*

- Sir Donald Nicholls VC concluded this by reference to analogy with the tort of negligence

- Reasoning not consistent with the approach of the COA in *Royscot.*

- Contributory negligence not available as a defence deceit *(Standard Chartered Bank v Pakistan National Shipping Corp (No. 2) [2002])*

1. **Innocent misrepresentation**

- Under common law, rule damages could not be given.

- Innocent misrepresentation not a tort

- Courts flexibility in applying this approach -

- Finding representation was a contractual term

- Or finding representation was enforceable as a **"collateral contract"**

Ex. De Lassalle v Guildford [1901] (collateral contract)
Facts

- Claimant was induced by representation that drains were fine on property to enter lease.

- Drains were not in good order – nothing in terms about the drainage.

Judgement

- Found representation warranty which was collateral to the lease

- There were essentially **2 contracts** between the parties: written lease and oral statement.

Need to seek out the existence of a collateral contract has been reduced by section 2(2) of the Misrepresentation Act 1967:

– "where a person has entered into a contract after a misrepresentation has been made to him otherwise than fraudulently, and he would be entitled, by reason of the misrepresentation, to rescind the contract, then, if it is claimed in any proceedings arising out of the contract, that the contract ought to be or has been rescinded, the court or arbitrator may declare the contract subsisting and award damages in lieu of recission, if of opinion that it would be equitable to do so, having regard to the nature of the misrepresentation and the loss that would be caused by it if the contract were upheld, as well as to the loss that recission would cause to the other party"

Section 2(2)

1. **The power to award damages is discretionary**

– contrast to section 2(1) where damages are available as of right
– not so under s2(2)

1. **Damages are in lieu of rescission**

– If the claimant wishes to rescind, can't get damages as well.

1. **Discretion of court is "broad one, to do what it is equitable"**

Wording of section 2(2) asks courts to investigate the *nature* of the misrepresentation
Courts most likely to invoke section 2(2) in a case where a representee has been induced by a misrepresentation to enter into what has turned out to be a *bad bargain for him*
Ex. *William Sindall plc v Cambridgeshire CC [1994]*
Facts

– Claimants bought land which dropped in value massively.

– Defendant innocently failed to disclose the existence of a private foul sere running across the land – the claimants believed this entitled them to withdraw from the contract.

Judgement

– COA - there had been no misrepresentation by the defendants

– If there was… would have exercised their discretion and granted the claimants damages in lieu of rescission. This was because claimant loss vs defendant loss was not comparable. (*UCB Corporate Services Ltd v Thomson [2005]*)

1. **The measure of damages to be awarded in lieu of rescission under section 2(2)**

– Tempting to give representee some protection for his reliance interest...

– Need to be cautious as the award of full reliance damages could protect the representee from his bad bargain.

– *COA (William Sindall) – no clear guidance on this point*

– **Hoffmann LJ** - damages under section 2(2) shouldn't be more than a sum which would have been awarded if the representation had been a warranty

– **Evans LJ** - the difference between the actual value received and the value which the property would have had if the representation had been true

Inability to rescind because of lapse of time

– Do claimants also lose the right to claim damages under section 2(2)?

The point is subject of a **conflict of authority**

– **Jacob J** *(Thomas Witter Ltd v TBP Industries Ltd)* – no don't lose it.

– **Judge Humphrey Lloyd QC** *(Floods of Queensferry Ltd v Shand Construction Ltd [2000])* - if lose right to rescind, the court has no jurisdiction to award damages under section 2(2)

– **Judge Jack QC** *(Zanzibar v British Aerospace (Lancaster House) Ltd [2002])* - agreed with Judge Humphrey Lloyd QC

Excluding liability for misrepresentation

– In common law, a person could not exclude liability for his own fraudulent misrepresentations *(S Pearson & Son Ltd v Dublin Corp [1907]) (HIH Casualty and General Insurance Ltd v Chase Manhattan Bank [2003])*

– At common law, however, a person could exclude liability for negligent or innocent misrepresentation – subject to interpretation:

Section 3 of the Misrepresentation Act 1967 (amended by Unfair Contract terms Act 1977, s8)

– limits the freedom of parties to exclude liability for the consequences of a misrepresentation

If a contract contains a term which would exclude or restrict -
(a) Any liability to which a party to a contract may be subject by reason of any misrepresentation made by him before the contract was made; or
(b) Any remedy available to another party to the contract by reason of such a misrepresentation that term shall be of no effect except in so far as it satisfies the requirement of reasonableness as stated in Section 1(1) of the Unfair Contract Terms Act 1977, and it is for those claiming that the term satisfies that requirement to show that it does

– Applies to business liability and bob-business liability

Ex. Raiffeisen Zentralbank Osterreich AG v Royal Bank of Scotland plc [2010]

– **Christopher Clarke J** - "the essential question is whether the clause in question goes to whether the alleged representation was made (or was intended to be understood and acted on as a representation), or whether it excludes or restricts liability in respect of representations made, intended to be acted on and in fact acted on; and that question is one of substance not form"

– Where the clause attempts "retrospectively to alter the character of what has gone before" or "to rewrite history or parts company with reality" then it is more likely to fall within the scope of Section 3 *(Springwell Navigation Corp v JP Morgan Chase Bank [2010])*

– Tricky test to apply.

– **Christopher Clarke J** - "to tell the man in the street that the car you are selling him is perfect and then agree that the basis of your contract is that no representations have been made or relied on, may be nothing more than an attempt retrospectively to alter the character and effect of what has gone far, and in substance an attempt to exclude or restrict liability".

8. Common Mistake and Frustration

Common mistake

- **Common mistake** - mistake common to both parties, agreement reached by parties is based upon a fundamentally mistaken assumption

- Court may nullify the consent of the parties and set aside the contract

Ex. Bell v Lever Brothers Ltd [1932]

Facts

- Defendants Bell and Snelling, contract with claimants and agreed to serve for 5 years as chairman and vice-chairman, of a subsidiary company of the claimants.

- One term stated: must not make any private profit for themselves.

- But defendants did, unbeknown to claimants.

- Claimants wanted to terminate the defendants' contracts.

- Created compensation agreements with the defendants; paying Bell £30,000 and Snelling £20,000.

- After paying, claimants discovered the breaches by the defendants

- Breaches would have allowed the claimants to terminate the service agreements without the payment of any compensation

- Claimants sought to recover the money

Judgement

- When they entered into the compensation agreements, the defendants did not have their breaches of duty in mind

- **Common mistake** that the service agreements were valid at the time of agreeing.

138

– House of Lords, by a majority of 3:2, held that the claimants could not recover the money

– **Lord Atkin** - The mistake was not sufficiently fundamental.

– **Lord Thankerton** - Test established by majority: "the common mistake must relate to something which both parties must necessarily have accepted in their minds as an essential element of the subject matter".

– Why was the claimants' mistake not fundamental? The payment of £50,000 to the defendants' in 1929, was a colossal sum of money.

– The answer to this question is not entirely clear. HoL appear to have wanted to limit claims to exceptional cases.

– This was an exceptional case - claimants had made a huge mistake.

Steyn J (Associated Japanese Bank (International) Ltd v Credit du Nord [1989]

– The mistake may not have been as important as it appears at first sight, as...

– The claimants were very anxious get rid of the men as soon as possible.

– May have contracted for compensation to achieve this even if they knew of breach.

MacMillan (2003)

– This hypothesis is unlikely

– The claim was brought by the claimants as a matter of principle.

– The failure of the claim is attributed to a number of different factors:

1. Mistake claim was added to main fraud claim as something of an afterthought

2. The claimants' fraud claim failed

3. Bell and Snelling made significant contributions to the success of the company, and the profit which they had made from their wrongdoing, were trifling in comparison with the benefits which the claimants received.

– Case statement that "a mistake must be fundamental in order to entitle a party to set aside a contract", must be read in context of the facts.

– Test adopted by the majority is a relatively open-textured.

Mistake as to the existence of the subject-matter of the contract

Mistake may be sufficiently fundamental to avoid a contract where both parties are mistaken as to the existence of the subject-matter of the contract
Ex. Galloway v Galloway (1914)
Facts

– Defendant, assuming wife had passed away, married the claimant

– Defendant and claimant later separated and entered a deed of separation under which the defendant agreed to pay a weekly allowance to the claimant

– The defendant subsequently discovered that his first wife was still alive and fell into arrears

– Claimant sued

Judgement

– Separation agreement was void on the ground that it was entered into under the common mistake that the parties were, in fact, married.

The sale of non-existent goods

– More complicated for sale of non-existent goods

Section 6 of the Sale of Goods Act 1979:

— "where there is a contract for the sale of specific goods, and the goods without the knowledge of the seller have perished at the time when the contract is made, the contract is void"

Ex. Couturier v Hastie (1856)
Facts

— The parties agreed contract for the sale of a cargo of corn.

— Before the contract was made, the corn had deteriorated to such an extent, that the master of the ship sold it — parties unaware.

— Seller argued that the buyer remained liable for the price of the corn.

Judgement

— H of L rejected the seller's argument

— Subject-matter of the contract was the corn, and since the corn did not exist, there was a total failure of consideration.

— Buyer not liable.

Principal interpretations which have been placed upon Couturier

1. **A mistake as to the existence of the subject-matter of a contract inevitably renders a contract void**

— This appears to be the interpretation placed upon Couturier by the draftsman of Section 6 of the Sale of Goods Act 1979

— But the word "mistake" was not used in any of the judgements in Couturier

— Court was principally concerned with the construction of the contract and the question whether the consideration had totally failed

— Court did not establish such an all-embracing proposition

1. **Contract void due to an implied condition precedent that the contract was capable of being performed (Denning LJ (Solle v Butcher [1950])**

— *Couturier* — the parties continued in agreement assuming the goods were actually capable of being sold, however, they were not, and the effect of the implied condition precedent was to render the contract void.

— Doesn't tell us why the courts will imply such a condition precedent.

1. **If contract is void will rest upon the construction of the contract**

— High Court of Australia in *McRae v Commonwealth Disposals Commission (1951)*
Facts

— The defendants tried to sell to the claimants the wreck of a tanker resting sunk on the Journal Reef; it was believed to contain oil.

— The claimants tried to salvage the vessel but could not find it

— It transpired the tanker had not ever existed
Judgement

— Claimants succeeded and got damages for breach.

— Defendants said there was no breach of contract because the alleged contract was void because of the non-existence of the subject-matter.

— Rejected.

— The defendants had promised the tanker existed, and the liability arose from the breach of this promise.

— In *Couturier,* there was a shared mistaken assumption.

— In contrast, in *McRae,* the defendants had promised the tanker existed.

— It was the defendant's who had assumed, through their promise, the risk of the tanker not existing.

Would English courts follow McRae?

- Result in *McRae* appears just since the defendants assumed the risk, and the result of the court's decision was to put this risk on the defendants

- In policy terms, there no issue that *McRae* should be followed *(Court of Appeal concluded this in Great Peace Shipping Ltd v Tsavliris Salvage (International) Ltd [2002]*

- Issue is reconciling *McRae* with *Section 6 of the Sale of Goods Act 1979*

- It could be argued that *McRae* would not be caught under the actual wording of section 6, because the tanker "never existed" and therefore it could not have "perished".

- Alternatively, it could be suggested that *section 6 is only a rule of construction which can, in a case such as McRae, be ousted by proof of contrary intention (Atiyah)*

- Problem with this argument is that, many sections of the Sale of Goods Act 1979, explicitly state that they are subject to contrary agreement.

- However, there is no such provision in section 6.

- Finally, although the main contract in a case such as McRae is void, the defendants could be liable under a collateral contract, with the terms here relating to whether the tanker was in existence.

- Consideration from claimants would be the entry into the void contract

- This being consideration can be doubted *(Strongman (1945) Ltd v Sincock [1955])* (more flexible approach to consideration adopted in *Williams v Roffey Bros & Nicholls (Contractors) Ltd [1991]*)

- Still feels artificial.

Mistake as to identity of the subject-matter

A mistake as to the identity of the subject-matter of the contract, could be sufficiently fundamental to void a contract if

both parties thought that they were dealing with one thing when they were actually dealing with another

> – No English case on this point *but Canadian case of Diamond v British Columbia Thoroughbred Breeder's Society (1966) may be of use.*

Mistake as to the possibility of performing the contract

A mistake may be sufficiently fundamental to void a contract if both parties believe the contract is capable of being performed when, in fact, it is not
Treitel divides into three categories:

Physical impossibility

Ex. Sheikh Brothers Ltd v Ochsner [1957]
Facts

> – The appellants gave respondents a licence to enter and cut sisal growing on their land
>
> – For this, the respondents agreed to provide the appellants 50 tons of cut sisal per month
>
> – Land was incapable of producing an average of 50 tons of sisal per month.
>
> – This fact was unbeknown to both parties to the contract.

Judgement

> – Privy council held that the contract was void because the mistake related to a matter which was essential to the agreement. In contracting the risk of the land not producing was not assumed by either party, it was simply not considered.

Legal impossibility

> – If the agreement requires something to be done which cannot, as a matter of law, be done.

Ex. Cooper v Phibbs (1867)
Facts

- The appellant took a lease of a salmon fishery from the respondents.

- Both parties believed the respondents had possession of the lease.

- The discovered the appellant, as the tenant in tail, was the owner of the fishery

Judgement

- Contract was set aside

- Court of Appeal *(Great Peace Shipping Ltd v Tsavliris Salvage (International) Ltd)* - "it is not easy to analyse the precise principles that led the House of Lords to set aside the agreement"

- Contract legally incapable of performance due to the appellant already being the owner of the fishery *(Great peace [110]: "the type of mistake under consideration was one whereby a party agrees to purchase a title which he already owns")*

Commercial impossibility

Ex. Griffith v Brymer (1903)
Facts

- Parties contracted for the hire of a room in order to watch the coronation procession of Edward VII

- Procession cancelled due to illness of Edward VII

- The parties had concluded their contract at 11 am, but unknown to both parties; the decision to operate on Edward VII was taken at 10am

Judgement

- Contract void, mistake of the parties went to the root or heart of contract.

- The cancellation of the procession undermined the commercial object of the contract.

- It did not matter that the contract was physically and legally capable of performance.

Mistake as to quality

A mistake as to quality of the subject-matter of the contract can be sufficiently fundamental to void the contract

- Courts very reluctant to find a mistake as to quality voids a contract, this can be shown in *Bell v Lever Brothers Ltd*

- Cases tricky to reconcile.

Ex. Leaf v International Galleries 1950

- Court of Appeal - sale agreement of a picture would not be void for mistake if both parties entered into the contract wrongly believing the picture to be a Constable.

Ex. Harrison and Jones v Burton and Lancaster [1953]
Facts

- Parties sale agreement for a specific brand of kapok, this was thought to be pure kapok.

- However, it had also contained some brush cotton; this made it worth much less.

Judgement

- Mistake was not sufficiently fundamental to avoid the contract

Ex. Oscar Chess Ltd v Williams [1957]
Facts

- Both parties entered into a contract for the sale of a car under the belief that the car was a 1948 model, when in fact it was a 1939 model

Judgement

- Mistake was not sufficiently fundamental to void the contract

Ex. Solle v Butcher [1950]

Facts

- Defendant contracted a lease agreement with the claimant, leasing a flat to the claimant for 7 years at a yearly fee of £250.

- This contract was agreed under the mistaken assumption that the flat was free from rent control.

- When this was discovered, with the legislation demanding only £140 per year, the claimant tried to recover the rent which he had overpaid

- The defendant counterclaimed for rescission of the lease on the ground of mistake

Judgement

- Court of Appeal held the landlord could set aside the lease "on terms".

- The judges all took different approaches

Jenkins LJ

- Dissented, arguing this was a mistake of law

- At that time this would not entitle the landlord to set aside the lease

- Mistake of law would now entitle the landlord to seek relief *(Brennan v Bolt Burden (a firm) [2004]*

Denning LJ

- The contract was valid at law but voidable in equity

Bucknill LJ

- The landlord could set aside the agreement because "there was a mutual mistake of fact on a matter of fundamental importance, namely, as to the identity of the flat".

Ex. Great Peace Shipping Ltd v Tsavliris Salvage (International) Ltd [2002]

Facts

- Defendant salvors contracted to provide salvage services for a vessel in the south Indian ocean.

- Defendants were told the Great Peace was in close proximity to the vessel in trouble, and so they contacted the claimants, who owned the Great Peace, by telephone.

- The parties agreed to hire it for a minimum of five days

- Great Peace was not as close to the stricken vessel as the defendants had been informed (410 miles away rather than 35 miles)

- When this was discovered, defendants tried to obtain the services of another vessel, which was not as far away

- Once they had done this, they tried to terminate the contract of hire with the claimants

Judgement

- Court of Appeal held that the mistake was not sufficiently fundamental to set aside the contract

- Despite the vessels being 410 miles apart, it would have taken them some 22 hours to meet; this delay was not enough to make performance "essentially different from those which the parties had envisaged when the contract was concluded".

- **mistake as to quality has been held to be sufficiently fundamental to void the contract...**

Ex. Scott v Coulson [1903]

- Sale of a life assurance policy was found to be void when, unknown to both parties, the assured had died, this mean the value of the policy had increased from £460 to £777

Ex. Nicholson and Venn v Smith-Marriott (1947)
Facts

- Defendants auctioned table napkins "with crest of Charles I and authentic property of that monarch".

— Relying on the description, the claimant won auction with bid of £787

— Later found out the napkin was only worth just over £100. Description was not accurate.

Judgement

— Hallet J - claimant could get damages for breach of contract

— Also found the claimant could void the contract o mistake

— Denning LJ in *Solle v Butcher* – weakens this case.

Can you reconcile the cases?

— General test seems relatively simple.

— Lord Thankerton *(Bell v Lever Brothers)* – mistake relate to an "essential and integral element of the subject matter of the contract".

— Problem is applying this to case facts.

Treitel's test

— Imagine you are able to "ask the parties, immediately after they made the contract, what its subject-matter was. If, in spite of the mistake, they would give the right answer the contract is valid at law".

— Helps us to understand the differences between *Oscar Chess* and *Nicholson and Venn*

— Doesn't seem to explain *Leaf*, parties here would have definitely said that they were purchasing a Constable, rather than simply a picture

— Test seems to provide useful guidance for mistake cases.

Different approach adopted by the Court of Appeal in *Great Peace*... **these elements must be present before a common mistake can void a contract:**

1. Common assumption about a state of affairs

2. No warranty by either party about that state of affairs

3. No fault of either party – in terms of the discrepancy between the state of affairs believed and in existence.

4. Non-existence of the state of affairs assumed must make performance of the contract impossible

5. The may be the existence, or a vital attribute, of the consideration to be provided or circumstances which must subsist if
   performance of the contractual adventure is to be possible

– Seems to suggest *the doctrine of common mistake operates within very
  narrow limits*

– Since-*Great Peace*, the Courts have applied requirements strictly

– The doctrine of mistake has been reduced, to point where its
  existence can be questioned *(Brennan v Bolt Burden (a firm)
  [2004]), (Champion Investments Ltd v Ahmed [2004]), and (Kyle Bay
  Ltd (trading as Astons Nightclub) v Underwriters Subscribing Under
  Policy 019057/08/01 [2007])*

– Authority exists supporting the idea that common mistake
  must be such as to render performance of the contract impossible *(Brennan v Bolt burden)*

– Not many mistakes with make performance impossible
  (Apvodedo NC v Collins]2008])

Mistake in equity

– Narrow approach in *Bell v Lever Brothers* was "supplemented by
  the more flexible doctrine of mistake in equity" *(Associated Japanese Bank (International) Ltd v Credit du Nord [1989])*

Mistake in equity differed in 3 major respects from mistake at law

Scope of the doctrine was wider

– Denning LJ (Solle v Butcher) - mistake in equity needs to be
  "fundamental", the party trying to set the contract aside must
  not themselves be "at fault".

- But courts can set aside contract, "whenever it is of the opinion that it is unconscientious for the other party to avail himself of the legal advantage which he has obtained".

- The wider test seemed to undermine certainty created in narrow test of *Bell v Lever Brothers*

Mistake in equity rendered a contract voidable and not void

In equity, courts had greater remedial flexibility

- Could set aside a contract 'on terms'.

- Courts could attach conditions to the entitlement of one party to set aside the initial contract

- Court of Appeal in *Great Peace* brought to an end this wider doctrine.

- The refusal of the COA in *Great Peace*, to follow the decisions made in *Solle v Butcher*, *Grist v Bailey* and *Magee v Pennine Insurance* controversial.

- COA can't as a rule refuse to follow its own decisions.

- Court said it was "impossible to reconcile *Solle v Butcher* with *Bell v Lever Brothers'* which is, of course, a decision of the House of Lords". This was used to justify the decision.

- "If coherence is to be restored to this area of our law, it can only be by declaring that there is no jurisdiction to grant recission of a contract on the ground of common mistake where that contract is valid and enforceable on ordinary principles of contract law".

- COA's decision in *Great Peace* seems to be correct

- *Solle v Butcher* and *Bell v Lever Brothers* were incompatible, simply not "conceivable that the House of Lords [in Bell v Lever brothers] overlooked an equitable right in Lever Bros to rescind the agreement, notwithstanding that the agreement was not void for mistake at common law".

— The H of L in *Bell v Lever Brothers,* wanted to find the agreement was valid and binding, and this was the result whether the claim was brought at law or equity

Court of Appeal observed in *Great Peace* (at [161]):

— "We can understand why the decision in *Bell v Lever Brothers Ltd,* did not find favour with Lord Denning. An equitable jurisdiction to grant recission on terms where a common fundamental mistake has induced a contract gives greater flexibility than a doctrine of common law which holds the contract void in such circumstances. Just as Law Reform (Frustrated Contracts) Act 1943 was needed to temper the effect of the common law doctrine of frustration, so there is scope for legislation to give greater flexibility to our law of mistake than the common law allows".

— The analogy with the Law Reform (Frustrated Contracts) Act 1943, is odd because the 1943 Act is concerned with regulating the remedial consequences of contracts already set aside.

Ex. Aikens J (Statoil ASA v Louis Dreyfus Energy Services LP [2008])

— Setting aside a contract for unilateral mistake...

— Aikens J rejected the argument that a wider equitable jurisdiction at common law

— Question of a *narrow doctrine of mistake* or a *more liberal regime*

— This is a question of certainty vs flexibility.

— *Bell v Lever Brothers* was a decision of certainty.

— *Great Peace* brings law back into line with this decision.

Frustration

— Mistake only relates to issues at the time of contracts.

— Event occurring after the contract has been formed are dealt with through the doctrine of frustration.

— *A contract frustrated where....* after contract formation, events happen which make performance of the contract impossible, illegal or something radically different from that which was in the contemplation of the parties at the time they entered into the contract

— Contract is ended by frustration. *(Hirji Mu LJi v Cheong Yue SS Co [1926])*

— This occurs regardless of the intention of the parties.

— Courts reluctant to use the doctrine.

Why are the courts cautious in invoking the doctrine of frustration?

Frustration, force majeure, and hardship

— 2 major reasons:

1. **The courts didn't want the doctrine to create an escape route for a party for whom the contract had become a bad bargain**

— *Lord Roskill* - the doctrine of frustration was "not lightly to be invoked to relieve contracting parties of the normal consequences of imprudent bargains" *(The Nema [1982])*

Ex. Davis Contractors Ltd v Fareham UDC [1956]
Facts

— Claimant builders contracted to build 78 houses for the defendants for a price of £94,000

— Work was to be completed in 8 months; however, there were shortages of skilled labour, and the work was 14 months over-schedule and cost £115,000.

— The claimants argued contract was frustrated.

Judgement

— Rejected by the House of Lords

— Lord Radcliffe - it was not "hardship or inconvenience or material loss itself which calls the principle of frustration into play. There must be as well such a change in the significance of the obligation that the thing undertaken would, if performed, be a different thing from that contracted for"

— *Davis* - clear rule and shows the contracting parties that, the courts will not manipulate deal to help party out of a bad bargain.

— Frustration still operates within narrow confines, will not be easily invoked *(Gold Group properties v BDW Trading Ltd [2010])*

— Supervising event must **radically** or **fundamentally** change the nature of performance: it cannot be used just because performance has become more onerous

How do courts decided if a contract has been frustrated?

— The courts use a **"multi-factorial"** approach *(Edwinton Commercial Corp, Global Tradeways Limited v Tsavliris Russ (Worldwide Salvage and Towage) Ltd (The "Sea Angel") [2007]*

Factors:
"Ex ante factors"

1. The terms of the agreement

2. The content of the contract, or its purpose.

3. The knowledge, expectations, assumptions of the parties — with a close regard placed on the assumption of risk.

Post-contractual
Islamic Republic of Iran Shipping Lines v Steamship Mutual Underwriting Association (Bermuda) Ltd [2010]

1. Nature of the event disrupting the contract

2. The parties' reasonable calculations about the possibilities of future performance after such an event.

— Must be a break in identity between the **contemplated** and the **new performance**, this will be difficult to establish. *(CTI Group Inc v Transclear SA [2008])*

2. Uncertainty of the future

- Contracting parties are expected to foresee and predict issues arising such as inflation, labour shortages or changes in interest rates at the time of contracting and protect against such changes within any agreement.

- **"force majeure"** clause may be used to cover for unexpected circumstances.

Ex. Channel Island Ferries Ltd v Sealink UK Ltd [1988] - contract between used force majeure clause:

- "A party shall not be liable in the event of non-fulfilment of any obligation arising under this contract by reason of Act of God, disease, strikes, lock-outs, fire, and any accident or incident of any nature beyond the control of the relevant party".

Hardship clause

- This clause will normally define what constitutes "hardship" and will set out a procedure if such hardship occurs.

- Generally, the clause will attempt to impose an obligation on both parties to use best efforts to renegotiate the contract in good faith – in order to mitigate any hardship.

Intervener clause

- Allows a third party to step in if hardship occurs and resolve the issue.

The advantages obtained by the use of such clauses?

1. **The provision of a degree of certainty**

2. **Frustration becomes very narrow**

- Give to the parties the opportunity, should they want to avail themselves of it, to agree that a wider class of events shall constitute *force majeure or hardship events*

- For example, price rises do not constitute a frustrating event (Davis Contractors v Fareham UDC)

– But a commercial contract could say that an "abnormal increase in prices and wages' shall constitute a force majeure event".

1. Parties can make provision for the consequences of the occurrence of the force majeure or hardship event

– Frustration can work too drastically.

– Parties may wish to adapt terms of existing contract to meet the new situation

– Doctrine of frustration doesn't allow for this.

– Must be remembered, in older cases once a party had assumed an obligation he was "bound to make it good" *(Paradine v Jane (1647)*

– This absolutist approach became more flexible (latter half of the 19th century), commencing with *Taylor v Caldwell (1863)* and ending with cases such as *Jackson v Union Marine Insurance Co Ltd (1874)* and *Krell v Henry [1903]* ...

– Courts now have reverted to a more restrictive approach

– Frustration is rare.

Frustration: a sterile doctrine?

– Doctrine remains capable of some form of development.

– House of Lords in *National Carriers v Panalpina (Northern) Ltd [1981]* expanded the scope.

– Was thought that the doctrine of frustration could not apply to a lease, because a lease created an interest in land and this interest would not be affected by the alleged frustrating event.

– *Panalpina* held that a lease could be frustrated

– Short term leases more likely to be frustrated.

– Decision demonstrated a willingness, to develop the doctrine of frustration

Impossibility

1. **A contract which has become impossible to perform is frustrated**

Ex. Taylor v Caldwell (1863)

Facts

- Defendants sold claimants a licence to use the "Surrey Gardens and Music Hall", for concerts at a rate of £100 per concert

- Before the first concert, the music hall burned down in an accident; it was now impossible to hold any concerts.

- The claimants claimed the defendants had breached the contract by not supplying the hall – tried to reclaim money spent on the concert marketing.

Judgement

- Contract was frustrated because fire had rendered performance of the contract impossible

- This event released both parties from their obligations under the contract.

1. **Partial destruction of the subject-matter may also frustrate a contract where it renders performance of the contract impossible**

Ex. Taylor v Caldwell

- "Surrey Gardens" as whole was not destroyed.

- Despite this, the fire at the music hall rendered performance of the contract impossible; the contract was frustrated as a result.

1. **Contracts for personal services are frustrated by the death of either party**

2. **Contract of employment may be frustrated if the ill-health leaves the employee permanently unfit for work**

3. **A contract may also be frustrated where the subject-matter of the contract is not available to perform contract.**

Ex. Bank Line Ltd v Arthur Capel & Co Ltd [1919]

— A charter party was frustrated when the ship was requisitioned

1. **Temporary unavailability of the subject-matter may also frustrate a contract**

Ex. Jackson v Union Marine Insurance Co Ltd (1874)
Facts

— A ship was chartered in November 1871, dispatched from Liverpool to Newport, here it was to be loaded with cargo for intended to go to San Francisco

— En route to Newport (January 1872), the ship was damaged, and a full repair was not completed until the end of August 1872.

Judgement

— Contract was frustrated

— It was simply not ready for the journey it had been contracted for.

— A voyage to San Francisco in late August 1872 was radically different from the intimal journey contemplated and agreed upon by the parties.

1. **The more disruption, the more likely it is that the contract will be frustrated**

Ex. The Nema [1982]

— A port was closed due to strikes. This meant only 2 of 7 contracted voyages could actually be completed.

Frustration of purpose

Where common purpose which the contract was entered into can no longer be carried out because of some supervening event, the contract can be frustrated

> — *Examples of frustration of purpose — very rare*....courts keen not to create an escape route for parties in bad bargains.

> — But rare example:

Ex. Krell v Henry [1903]
Facts

> — Defendant hired a flat in Pall Mall for two-day period from the claimant.

> — Object of contract was to watch the coronation procession of Edward VII.

> — This was not expressly acknowledged within the contract.

> — Coronation postponed due to King's illness. This postponement occurred after the contract had been formed.

Judgement

> — Contract was frustrated

However,....
Ex. Herne Bay Steam Boat Co v Hutton [1903]
Facts

> — The defendant hired the claimant's ship "for the purpose of viewing the naval review and for a day's cruise around the fleet".

> — Naval review cancelled due to King's illness.

Judgement

> — Contract not frustrated

Comparison with Krell?

- Look at example considered by Vaughan Williams LJ *(Krell)*

- It was put to Vaughan Williams LJ that, if the contract was frustrated in *Krell*, then it:

- "would follow that if a cabman was engaged to take someone to Epsom on Derby Day at a suitably enhanced price for such a journey... both parties to the contract would be discharged in the contingency of the race at Epsom for some reason becoming impossible".

- But Vaughan Williams LJ said this contract would not be frustrated because he did not think that "the happening of the race would be the foundation of the contract".

- In *Krell*, "the foundation of the contract" was watching the coronation.

- *Krell contract was extremely unusual.*

- Rooms were hired out by the day, excluding the night, and only purpose which both parties had in entering the contract, was to hire the rooms for viewing the coronation

- In *Herne Bay Steamboat Co v Hutton* - defendant could still view the fleet, although the defendant's motive in entering into the contract might have been to see the naval review

- It could not be said that that was the "common foundation of the contract".

- Similar reasoning explains the example of the cancellation of the Derby - "common foundation" idea crucial.

- *Krell* very narrow decision

- Scope will not be broadened (*North Shore Ventures Ltd v Anstead Holdings Inc [2010]*), has been distinguished rather than followed (*Amalgamated Investment and Property Co Ltd v John Walker & Sons Ltd [1977]*)

Illegality

Supervening illegality can operate to frustrate a contract
Ex. Fibrosa Spolka Akcyjna v Fairbairn Lawson Combe Barbour Ltd [1943]
Facts

- The respondents agreed to make machines for appellants and deliver them to Gdynia in Poland

- Gdynia then became occupied by the German Army

Judgement

- Contract was frustrated, in wartime against the law to trade with the enemy

- Physical possibility of manufacture and delivery not as important.

- Public policy considerations

- Need to ensure the law is observed (Islamic Republic of Iran Shipping Lines v Steamship Mutual Underwriting Association (Bermuda) Ltd [2010])

- Where illegality is only temporary/partial - the contract will be frustrated only if the illegality affects the performance of the contract in a substantial or fundamental way (Contrast: *Denny, Mott & Dickinson v James B Fraser & Co Ltd [1944]* and *Cricklewood Property Investment Trust Ltd v Leighton's Investment Trust Ltd [1945]*

Express provision

Limitations on frustration doctrine:

1. **No frustration where the parties have made express provision for the occurrence of the event which supposedly frustrates the contract** *(Joseph Constantine Steamship Line Ltd v Imperial Smelting Corp Ltd [1942])*

- In public policy cases frustration can operate despite express provision in the contract *(Ertel Bieber and Co v Rio Tinto Co Ltd [1918]*

Ex. Metropolitan Water Board v Dick, Kerr and Co [1918]- a restrictive approach:
Facts

- Contractors agreed to construct a reservoir in 6 years

- Contract stated, in the event of a delay "whatsoever and how-soever occasioned", the contractors were to apply to the engineer for extension.

Judgement

- Government Order forced contractors to stop the work and sell the plant,

- Held the contract was frustrated

- Delay clause was not intended to apply to this type of fundamental change.

- Intention was merely to contract for procedure in relation to temporary difficulties.

- It did not cover fundamental changes to contract (*Jackson v Union Marine Insurance Co Ltd*)

- Result = extremely difficult, if not impossible, to draft a force majeure clause which has the effect of absolutely removing possibility of frustration.

- In *Metropolitan Water Board* case, even the widest of clauses may be held not to encompass certain events.

Foreseen and foreseeable events

- Doctrine is about unforeseen events.

Ex. Walton Harvey Ltd v Walker and Homfrays Ltd [1931]
Facts

- The defendant granted to the claimant the right to advertise for 7 years on the defendant's hotel.

- Council then compulsorily purchased hotel and knocked it down.

Judgement

- Event was within the contemplation of the defendant.

But... the proposition that a foreseeable event cannot frustrate a contract has been challenged...

Ex. Lord Denning (The Eugenia [1964])

– An event is foreseeable only where it is one which "any person of ordinary intelligence would regard as likely to occur"*(Treitel)*

– The question would appear to be one of fact and degree

Ex. Rix LJ (The Sea Angel [2007])

– "the less that an event, in its type and its impact, is foreseeable, the more likely it is to be a factor which, depending on other factors in the case, may lead onto frustration".

– Rix LJ also warned against the "over refinement" of submissions.

Self-induced frustration

A party cannot claim frustration where the alleged frustrating event occurs through his own conduct

– consequences of concluding that the frustration was self-induced:

– Frustration usually claimed as a defence to an action or for breach of contract

– So, where frustration is "self-induced" will often see a finding of breach.

– Despite the concept of self-induced frustration being clearly established in the cases, the courts have never established its limits with any degree of clarity

Ex .Hobhouse J - J Lauritzen AS v Wijsmuller BV (The Super Servant Two) [1989]

– Self-induced frustration is a "label" used to describe "those situations where one party has been held by the courts not to be entitled to treat himself as discharged from his contractual obligations".

- Negligence by the defendant also amounts to self-induced frustration, because this event is not "altogether outside the control of the defendant".

- It is within his control, notwithstanding the fact that his negligence is a result of his unreasonable failure to exercise that control (*Joseph Constantine Steamship Line Ltd v imperial Smelting Corp Ltd [1942]*)

The scope of self-induced frustration can be seen in the following cases....

Ex. Maritime National Fish Ltd v Ocean Trawlers Ltd [1935]
Facts

- The defendants chartered a ship from the claimants,

- Ship could only be used for its intended purpose if it was fitted with an otter trawl

- Otter trawl needed licence, defendants given 3 licences

- Chose not to apply licence to the chartered ship. Instead used them on ships they already owned.

- Defendants denied liability to pay contract under terms on the ground that the contract had been frustrated by their failure to obtain a licence

Judgement

- Case of self-induced frustration

Ex. J Lauritzen AS v Wisjmuller BV (The Super Servant Two) [1990]
Facts

- Defendants agreed to transport the claimants' oil rig using, at their option, Super Servant One or Super Servant two.

- Defendants decided to allocate Super Servant Two to the performance of the contract with the claimants, and allocate Super Servant One to the performance of other concluding contracts

- Super Servant Two sank after formation.

164

– Contract could not be performed by Super Servant One, due to its allocation to the performance of other concluded contracts.

– Contract was performed by another more expensive means.

Judgement
Defendants denied liability on two grounds:

1. The contract had been frustrated as a result of the sinking of Super Servant Two (argument rejected)

– COA - cause of the non-performance was the choice of the defendants to allocate Super Servant one to the performance of other contracts, rather than sinking.

– Self-induced frustration.

– Conclusion of the COA leaves a seller in an impossible position where source of supply partially fails due to an unforeseen event

Counter argument

– Problem, the defendants had no real choice as to the allocation of Super Servant One

– It was impossible to allocate it to the performance of all concluded contracts, and so the sinking of Super Servant Two compelled them to make such a decision

1. Could terminate contract without incurring any liability under the terms of a force majeure clause

– One of the force majeure events listed in the contract was "perils or dangers and accidents of the sea".

– COA - this phrase was apt to encompass the sinking of Super Servant Two

– Provided there was no negligence clause was effective defence to the claimants' claim for damages

– *Super Servant Two* shows narrow confines of frustration and use of a well-drafted force majeure clause in a contract

The effects of frustration

- A contract which is discharged on the ground of frustration is brought to an end automatically at the time of the frustrating event

Ex. Fibrosa Spolka Akcyjna v Fairbairn Lawson Combe Barbour Ltd [1943]

- Money paid prior to the frustration recoverable upon a total failure of consideration

- *Fibrosa* - appellants sought to recover £1000 they had paid to the respondents on the signing of the contract

- H of L - consideration for the payment had wholly failed because the machines had not been delivered to the appellants and that they were entitled to the recovery of their payment

2 principal defects remained:

1. The payer could only recover money paid upon a total failure of consideration; where failure partial he couldn't recover *(Whincup v Hughes (1871),*

2. The payee couldn't set off against the money to be repaid any expenditure incurred.

Rectified by the enactment of **Section 1(2) of the Law Reform (Frustrated Contracts) Act 1943**

Effect of this subsection is threefold

1. Moneys paid before frustrating event recoverable

2. Sums payable before discharge cease to be payable

3. The payee can set off against the sums so paid expenses which he has incurred before the time of discharge in performance of contract.

Section 1(2) meets 2 deficiencies of the common law

1. Right to recover money is not confined to a total failure of consideration

2. The payee can set off against the sums repayable any reliance expenditure which he had incurred in the performance of the contract.

Deficiencies which remain within Section 1 (2)

1. **Not clear how the court is to calculate the amount of expenditure which a payee is entitled to retain**

— All of expenditure? A proportion?

Ex. Gamerco SA v ICM/Fair Warning (Agency) Ltd [1995]

— Garland J - "no indication in the Act, the authorities or the relevant literature that the court is obliged to incline towards either total retention or equal division".

— Court must find "justice in a situation which the parties had neither contemplated nor provided for, and to mitigate the possible harshness of allowing all loss to lie where it has fallen"

— "broad nature" of the discretion

1. **The payee cannot recover or retain more than the value of the repayment**

— Any reliance expenditure more than the prepayment cannot be recovered under section 1 (2)

— Might be recoverable under section 1 (3) where the expenditure results in a valuable benefit being obtained by the other party (see below).

The effects of frustration upon a claim to recover the value of goods supplied or services provided prior to the frustrating event

Ex. Appleby v Myers (1867)
Facts

— Claimants contracted to fit machinery in the defendants' factory and for 2 years maintenance.

— Payment was to be made on completion of the work

- An accidental fire destroyed the factory and machinery.

- Frustrated contract.

Judgement

- Claimants only entitled to payment when performance was completed (entire obligations/entire contracts rule)

- This rule caused hardship to the provider of services under a frustrated contract

It has been hence replaced by **section 1 (3) of the Law Reform (Frustrated Contracts) Act 1943**, which states:

- "where any party to the contract has, by reason of anything done by any other party thereto in, or for the purpose of, the performance of the contract, obtained a valuable benefit (other than a payment of money to which the last foregoing subsection applies) before the time of discharge, there shall be recoverable from him by the said other party such sum (if any), not exceeding the value the said benefit to the party obtaining it, as the court considers just, having regard to all the circumstances of the case and, in particular -

- the amount of any expenses incurred before the time of discharge by the benefited party in, or for the purpose of, the performance of the contract, including any sums paid or payable by him to any other party in pursuance of the contract and retained or recoverable by that party under the last foregoing subsection, and

- the effect, in relation to the said benefit, of the circumstances giving rise to the frustration of the contract

This subsection is an **unnecessarily complex provision**
Basic effect of subsection:

- "Where one party to the contract has conferred upon the other party a "valuable benefit", (other than a payment of money which is governed by s 1 (2)) before the time of discharge, he shall be entitled to recover a "just sum" which shall not exceed

168

the value of the benefit which he has conferred upon the other party"

Ex. BP v Hunt [1979]

Robert Goff J - 2 steps involved in a section 1(3) claim

1. The identification and valuation of the benefit

– No definition of what counts as a benefit: the value of the services performed or the end product of the services

– In *BP v Hunt (Robert Goff J)* in an "appropriate case", it was the end product

However, there are 2 circumstances in which a court could have regard to the value of the services in identifying the benefit:

1. Where the service by its very nature does not result in a product (e.g., the transportation of goods)

2. Where the service results in an end product which has no objective value (e.g., a claimant who commences the redecoration, to the defendant's execrable taste, of rooms which are in good decorative order)

The word "benefit" has unfortunate consequences

– In cases such as *Appleby v Myers*, it means that the result would be unaffected by the Act because the claimants' work was destroyed by fire – no end product

2. The assessment of a "just sum"

– Robert Goff J - the contractual allocation of risk always relevant to deciding what is a just sum

– Robert Goff J - measure of certainty by stating that the aim ought to be "the prevention of the unjust enrichment of the defendant at the [claimant's] expense' and that the assessment should, therefore, be similar to that undertaken by a court in a *quantum merit* claim."

Lawton LJ (COA - BP v Hunt [1982])

– Rejected by Lawton LJ

– He stated "what is just is what the trial judge thinks is just"

– Discretion of the trial judge

– Can be concluded that section 1(3) is poorly drafted.

9. Duress, Undue Influence, Inequality of Bargaining Power

Introduction

- Law of contract has always limited the extent to which parties to a contract can exploit and rely on their economic power.

- Duress and undue influence have sought to achieve this.

- Recent effort to introduce into the common law a doctrine of inequality of bargaining power

- English courts have given up on this doctrine. But, the **Unfair Terms in Consumer Contracts Regulations (1999),** which give have given the courts substantial powers to regulate unfair terms for consumer contracts.

Common law duress

- No trouble for courts in setting aside a contract on the ground of duress to the person

- More difficult to establish duress to goods or economic duress.

- Doctrine of consideration was of some use here.

Example

- If Tom puts a gun to John's head and extracts from John a promise to pay him £10,000, then Johns obligations are unenforceable because Tom did not provide any consideration for such a promise.

- But doctrine of consideration isn't well equipped to deal with duress, because of the rule that consideration must be sufficient but need not be adequate

- Thus, if Tom offers and agrees to give his pencil, worth just £1, consideration is provided for the promise to pay £10,000.

— *Williams v Roffey Bros & Nicholls (Contractors) Ltd [1991]* — COA reduces scope for consideration to act as a tool to prevent duress.

— COA - modern courts will be more willing to find consideration in the renegotiation of a contract and duress will concern just the fairness of the renegotiation

— *Ex. Stilk v Myrick (1809)* - reclassified as a duress case.

— Post - *Williams v Roffey Bros* - greater significance for duress.

— Confusion with duress is identifying its limits.

Now, the **scope of the doctrine of duress at common law must be considered**

3 Types of duress

Duress to the person

— Actual violence or threats to claimant or members of claimant's family.

Ex. Barton v Armstrong [1976]

— Privy Council - threats don't have to be the sole reason for contracting.

— Need only be a factor influencing the victim.

Duress to goods

— Threat of damage to the victim's goods.

— Old case of *Skeate v Beale (1840)* — found unlawful detention of another's goods does not constitute duress — this has prevented doctrine from developing.

— But, authority for argument that money paid to release goods unlawfully detained was recoverable; *(Astley v Reynolds (1731))*

— *Skeate v Beale* criticised.

Ex. The Siboen and the Sibotre [1976]

— Kerr J refused to follow *Skeate v Beale*

The Evia Luck [1992]

- Due to the development of the doctrine of economic duress, it can be predicted that Skeate v Beale will not be followed today

- **Lord Goff** - the limitation in *Skeate v Beale*, that only duress to the person would entitle a party to avoid a contract, had been discarded

Economic duress

- Economic duress arises where one party exploits superior economic position in an "illegitimate" way - to coerce another to agree to terms.

- Recognised by Kerr J in *The Siboen and The Sibotre*

Lord Hoffmann - two wrongs of duress:

1. **"Pressure amounting to compulsion of the will of the victim"**

2. **"Illegitimacy of the pressure"**

- Traditionally, "compulsion of the will of the victim" was known as "coercion of the will of the victim", which was such as to vitiate his consent

- "Coercion of the will" see in early economic duress cases *(The Siboen and The Sibotre)*

- The "coercion of the will" theory has been criticised by Professor Atiyah.

- Duress doesn't take away a person's choice but instead presents him with a choice between evils.

- If I am forced to contract at gunpoint – I most definitely make the choice to contract, I choose not to be shot, and in doing so I do actively choose to contract. My consent is very real.

- What is wrong with this situation is not my lacking in consent, but rather how my consent was obtained.

- Criticism followed by the courts.

- **Lord Goff (The Evia Luck)**- doubted whether "it is helpful to speak of the claimant's will having been coerced".

- Lord Hoffmann in *R v A-G for England and Wales* shows courts have not yet abandoned the language of "compulsion of the will" entirely

- More modern approach has regard to the consent of the claimant only to ensuring that there is a sufficient causal link between the pressure applied by the defendant and the entry into contract

- But there is uncertainty as to the test for this.

- Duress to the person - the threat need only be one cause, and there is a suggestion in *Barton v Armstrong,* that onus of proof switches to defendant to show their pressure had no effect.

- Clear this generous approach to the claimant doesn't apply in cases of economic duress. Would be too easy to get relief.

- More serious challenge in establishing economic duress. Not entirely clear how significant the obstacles to finding this duress are.

- Onus of proof is on the claimant to prove the *existence of a sufficient causal link* (Huyton SA v Peter Cremer GmbH & Co Inc [1999]) and the claimant must also show that the pressure applied was a "significant cause" inducing him to enter into the contract *(The Evia Luck [1992])* or even a "but for" cause *(Kolmar Group AG v Traxpo Enterprises Pty Ltd [2010])*

Court's consideration

Courts also likely to consider whether or not there was an alternative for claimant.

Ex. Huyton SA v Peter Cremer GmbH & Co Inc

- **Mance J** - while it was "not necessary to go so far as to say that it is an inflexible third essential ingredient of economic duress that there should be no or no practical alternative course open to the innocent party".

- It seemed to him "self-evident that relief may not be appropriate, if an innocent party decides, as a matter of choice, not to pursue an alternative remedy which any and possibly some other reasonable persons in his circumstances would have pursued".

Consent role in:

— Differentiating between duress and a settlement of an honest claim *(Pao On v Lau Yiu Long [1980])*

— *Movement towards shifting focus onto the pressure applied:*

Ex. DSDN Subsea Ltd v Petroleum Geo-Services ASA [2000]

— **Dyson J** - "in determining whether there has been illegitimate pressure, the court takes into account a range of factors. These include whether there has been an actual or threatened breach of contract; whether the person allegedly exerting the pressure had acted in good or bad faith; whether the victim had any real practical alternative but to submit to the pressure; whether the victim protested at the time; and whether he affirmed and sought to rely on the contract. These are all relevant factors. Illegitimate pressure must be distinguished from the rough and tumble of the pressures of normal commercial bargaining".

flexible approach problems

— Uncertainty.

— Preferable to try to find a more precise and certain definition of illegitimate.

— Can be achieved by categorising distinct types of illegitimacy

— **Lord Hoffmann** *(R v A-G for England and Wales [2003]*- the legitimacy of the pressure must be examined from "2 aspects":

1. The nature of the pressure

2. The nature of the demand which the pressure is applied to support

— "Generally speaking, the threat of any form of unlawful action will be regarded as illegitimate. on the other hand, the fact that the threat is lawful does not necessarily make the pressure legitimate".

– **Lord Atkin** *(Thorne v Motor Trade Association [1937])* - "The ordinary blackmailer normally threatens to do what he has a perfect right to do - namely, communicate some compromising conduct to a person whose knowledge is likely to affect the person threatened... What he has to justify is not the threat but the demand of money".

Privy Council

Pricy Council thus appeared to envisage a 2-stage approach to illegitimacy

1. **Unlawful threat = generally duress**

2. **Lawful threat is used to support a demand which is unlawful= may constitute duress**

– Unlawful threats, normally easy to categorise. *(Pao On v Lau Yiu Long)*

– When pressure is a threatened breach of contract more difficult.

– Caution from courts, not every threat to breach is duress.

– Possible only bad faith breaches of contract will be classified as illegitimate for this purpose

– More difficult than this is the case where pressure is not in itself unlawful

– Tempting to say cannot be duress if threat is lawful.

– **Lord Hoffmann** - observed that it is necessary to extend the category of illegitimacy, to catch the case of blackmail, where the threat itself is lawful but it is used to attain a goal which is unlawful *(Lord Scarman - Universe Tankships of Monrovia v International Transport Workers' Federation [1983])*

– But blackmail is, however, the exception, not the rule

– General rule = defendant who threatens to do what he is entitled to do will not be held to have applied illegitimate pressure

– Refusal to waive existing contractual obligations, not duress. *(Alec Lobb (Garages) Ltd v Total oil (GB) Ltd [1983])*

– Demands for payment by owner of goods (Who has terminated a hire-purchase contract), as the price for not exercising his right to repossess the goods doesn't amount to duress *(Alf Vaughan & Co Ltd v Royscot Trust plc [1999])*

– Equally, threat to refuse to contract shouldn't constitute duress because no wrongful threat is made in refusing to contract.

– Must be qualified:

Ex. CTN Cash and Carry Ltd v Gallaher Ltd [1994]

– COA - threat to refuse to contract did not constitute duress

– Court emphasised the fact that the party applying the pressure did not act in bad faith.

– So, position may change if there is bad faith

– But in such a case, it may be possible to say that there has been illegitimate pressure

– **Steyn LJ** – did not say can "never be a case of lawful act duress" in a commercial context

– Supported in PC in *Borelli v Ting [2010]*

Difficulty *where the duress is alleged to take the form of a threatened breach of contract*

– Need for illegitimate threat, leads to the conclusion that a break of a contract can constitute duress - but refusal to waive an existing contractual obligation cannot

– Difficult to apply.

– Can't' say all threatened breaches of contract count as the application of illegitimate pressure: an additional element should be required

– Burrows (2010) - argued that bad faith must be important in deciding whether or not a threatened breach is illegitimate *(Mance J - Huyton SA v Peter Cremer GmbH & Co Inc)*

– But, what constitutes bad faith?

— Burrows - "a threatened breach of contract should be regarded as illegitimate if concerned to exploit the claimant's weakness rather than solving financial or other problems of the defendant".

To this general test, Burrows adds **2 supplementary clarificatory ideas**:

1. A threat shouldn't be illegitimate if the threat is a reaction to circumstances that nearly constitute frustration

2. A threat not illegitimate if it merely corrects what was always clearly a bad bargain

— Problem, English law doesn't invoke notions of bad faith in the context of breach of contract.

— Bad faith focus in *CTN Cash and Carry Ltd v Gallaher Ltd* - can be distinguished on the ground that a refusal to contract is not in itself wrongful, so that bad faith might used to lean towards finding of "illegitimacy".

— However, a threatened breach of contract is already wrongful.

— Intermediate approach used by Christopher Clarke J (Kolmar Group AG v Traxpo Enterprises Pty Ltd) — concludes, a "threat to break a contract will generally be regarded as illegitimate, particularly where the defendant must know that it would be in breach of contract if the threat were implemented"

— Under this reasoning, a breach threatened in bad faith, more likely to be duress.

— Good faith threat could amount to duress in certain context:

Williams v Roffey Bros

— Duress not pleaded in the case.

— Difficult to understand why: was a potential breach of contract by the sub-contractors and probability of that breach was a cause of the main contractors offering to pay more.

— Some people feel content with conclusion that there was **no duress** – based on facts:

The reason for this is because...

1. **The main contractors called the meeting and who made the offer to pay more**

2. **The claimant was obviously incompetent**

— Couldn't supervise workers or cost job.

— But, sub-contractor deliberately priced the job very low so that he was awarded the contract, then made it clear to the main contractor that he was unlikely to complete on time unless offered money.

— Sounds like duress.

Difficult distinction between the incompetent sub-contractor (Williams v Roffey Bros) and contractor who deliberately under-prices the job?

— Additional factor, like bad faith, could be used to help here?

— Or conclude that all breaches of contract are illegitimate and that a crucial error was made in *Williams v Roffey Bros* in not arguing for duress?

Contract which is entered into duress is voidable

— **Lord Saville** *(Borelli v Ting)* - agreement entered through duress "is not valid as a matter of law".

— Fact that duress renders a contract voidable but not void - has consequence that the party alleging duress must to take steps to set aside agreement.

— If this is not done within a reasonable time, can lead to the conclusion that the agreement has been affirmed and can no longer be set aside *(North Ocean Shipping Co Ltd v Hyundai Construction Co Ltd [1979])*

179

Undue influence

— Equitable doctrine

— Precise meaning of undue influence not yet clear.

What does undue mean?

— Illegitimate?

— Does it mean too much?

What does influence mean?

— Is influence relating to pressures or is a subtler form of dominating a contracting party? Case law hasn't answered this question.

2 views:

Focus in these cases:

1. Claimant's position, impairment on their decision making and the extent to which this impacted upon the bargain.

2. Requires some wrongful conduct on the part of the defendant

— Considerations: "abuse" of a position of confidence, the "exploitation" of a party's impairment, "advantage taking" in another form.

— No single view from the courts as to the dominant factor.

— In recent cases, however, certain Judges have placed emphasis on the **need for some "wrongful" conduct on the part of the defendants**

Lord Hoffmann (R v A-G for England and Wales [2003])

— "like duress at common law, undue influence is based upon the principle that a transaction to which consent has been obtained by unacceptable means should not be allowed to stand. Undue influence has concentrated in particular upon the unfair exploitation by one party of a relationship which gives him ascendancy or influence over the other"

- Notice "unacceptable means" and "unfair exploitation" are heavily focussed on the defendant's actions.

Lord Millett (National Commercial Bank (Jamaica) Ltd v Hew [2003]

- "Undue influence is one of the grounds on which equity intervenes to give redress where there has been some unconscionable conduct on the part of the defendant... the doctrine involves two elements. First, there must be a relationship capable of giving rise to the necessary influence. And secondly, the influence generated by the relationship must have been abused".

Norris J (Davies v AIB Group (UK) plc [2012])

- Undue influence "does not protect against folly, but against victimisation" and that it has a "connotation of impropriety".

Case law not entirely consistent:

Mummery LJ (Pesticcio v Huet [2004])

- Defendant's wrongdoing not an essential component?
- "Although undue influence is sometimes described as an "equitable wrong" or even as a species of equitable fraud, the basis of the court's intervention is not the commission of a dishonest or wrongful act by the defendant, but that, as a matter of public policy, the presumed influence, arising from the relationship of trust and confidence should not operate to the disadvantage of the victim, if the transaction is not satisfactorily explained by ordinary motives: *Allcard v Skinner (1887)*. The court scrutinises the circumstances in which the transaction, under which benefits were conferred on the recipient, took place and the nature of the continuing relationship between the parties, rather than any specific act or conduct on the part of the recipient. A transaction may be set aside by the court, even though the actions and conduct of the person who benefits from it could not be criticised as wrongful"

Court may look to both claimant's *position* and the defendant's *actions:*

181

— Both ideas considered in *Randall v Randall [2004]* and *Turkey v Ahwad [2005]*

— Most cases do involve some wrongdoing. However, possible to imagine cases where this is not present.

— **Mummery LJ** – no wrongdoing from Mother Superior in *Allcard v Skinner*

— She has not ensured claimant got independent advice, rather than actively committing a wrong. This advice would have allowed the claimant to make a more informed decision before giving away all her property on entering the order.

— Decision in *Allcard* - relates to the claimant's excessive dependence, rather than wrongdoing.

— Unwise to categorise undue influence as entirely dependent on actions of a defendant.

Ex. *Royal Bank of Scotland v Etridge [2001]*

— Not likely H of L intended to shut the door completely on a conception of undue influence entirely reliant on defendant's actions.

— Lordships noted many forms of undue influence (coercion, domination, victimisation and other "unacceptable forms of persuasion") and the perils of merely focussing on defendant's actions.

Traditional approach is to divide undue influence in 2 distinct categories

1. **Presumed undue influence**

2. **Actual undue influence**

— Result of the decision of the H of L in *Etridge*

— Used to be substantial due to "manifest disadvantage" requirement applied in the case of presumed undue influence (*National Westminster Bank plc v Morgan [1985]*)

— This was not needed for actual undue influence (*CIBC Mortgage plc v Pitt [1994]*)

- Disadvantage manifest if "it would have been obvious as such to any independent and reasonable persons who considered the transaction at the time with knowledge of all the relevant facts" *(Bank of Credit and Commerce International SA v Aboody [1990])*

- But the "manifest disadvantage" requirement underwent judicial reconsideration in *Etridge.*

- **Lord Nicholls** - "the exercise of undue influence is unlikely to occur, where the transaction is innocuous".

- Seems to lean towards a disadvantage requirement?

Actual undue influence overlap with common law duress

- **Lord Nicholls** *(Etridge)* - actual undue influence "comprises overt acts of improper pressure or coercion such as unlawful threats" and thus there is today "much overlap with the principle of duress as this principle has subsequently developed".

Ex. Williams v Bayley (1866)
Facts

- Father tried to rescind a mortgage executed in favour of a banker.

- He demonstrated he had created the mortgage as a result of his fear induced through the banker's warning or threat that he had it in his power to prosecute his son.

Judgement

- Could rescind the mortgage on the ground of undue influence

But... today *Williams v Bayley* can be viewed as a **duress case**

- Where the actual undue influence is actually illegitimate pressure, suggested there should be no requirement for a claimant to prove that the transaction cannot reasonably be accounted for on ordinary motives.

- No requirement for duress, so why should there be for undue influence?

— Cases of actual undue influence extend beyond mere "pressure cases".

— Lord Hobhouse *(Etridge)* - actual undue influence was "an equitable wrong committed by the dominant party against the other which makes it unconscionable for the dominant party to enforce his legal rights against the other"

— Wider conception of undue influence seems to encompass cases in which the claimant can prove that the defendant has in fact taken advantage of, or abused, a relationship of trust.

Presumed undue influence cases are even more problematic

— But H of L *(Etridge)* - introduced caution into this area of the law, and has discouraged parties from relying upon it.

— Such scepticism with regards to the utility of the presumption was apparent in the speech of Lord Clyde

— **Lord Clyde** - "there is... room for uncertainty whether the presumption is of the existence of an influence or of its quality as being undue" ... "At the end of the day, after trial, there will either be proof of undue influence or that proof will fail and it will be found that there was no undue influence".

— Presumption has not been abandoned altogether.

— It has been retained. But, shift in the evidential onus of proof:

— **Lord Nicholls** - "proof that the complaint placed trust and confidence in the other party in relation to the management of the complainant's financial affairs, coupled with a transaction which calls for explanation, will normally be sufficient, failing satisfactory evidence to the contrary, to discharge the burden of proof".

3 elements to a case of "presumed undue influence"

1. **The claimant must prove that he placed trust and confidence in the defendant for management of their affairs.**

— Law presumes the existence of a relationship of trust and confidence

- **Lord Nicholls** (Etridge) - certain relationships where "the law presumes, irrebuttably, that one party had influence over the other".

- Relationship within this class are "parent and child, guardian and ward, trustee and beneficiary, solicitor and client, and medical adviser and patient" and also spiritual adviser and disciple *(Curtis v Curtis [2011])*

- Husband and wife – no.

- If falling outside the category, a claimant must show they actually reposed trust and confidence in the defendant.

1. **Claimant must prove that the transaction "calls for explanation"**

- Reformation of "manifest disadvantage" requirement (Lord Scarman - *National Westminster Bank plc v Morgan [1985]*)

- **Lord Nicholls** *(Etridge)* - "experience has... shown that this expression (manifest disadvantage) can give rise to misunderstanding" and has been "causing difficulty".

- Lord Nicholls going back to test by Lindley LJ (Allcard v Skinner (1887)) - "whether the gift is so large that it cannot be accounted for on the ground of friendship, relationship, charity or other ordinary motives on which ordinary men act".

- Change one of title rather than substance

Lord Nicholls observed:

- "it would be absurd for the law to presume that every gift by a child to a parent, or every transaction between a client and his solicitor or between a patient and his doctor, was brought about by undue influence unless the contrary is affirmatively proved. Such a presumption would be too-far-reaching. The law would be out of touch with everyday life if the presumption were to apply to every Christmas or birthday gift by a child to a parent, or to an agreement whereby a client or patient agrees to be responsible for the reasonable fees of his legal or medical adviser. The law would be rightly open to ridicule, for transactions such as these are unexceptionable.

They do not suggest that something may be amiss. So something more is needed before the law reverses the burden of proof, something which calls for an explanation. When that something more is present, the greater the disadvantage to the vulnerable person, the more cogent must be the explanation before the presumption will be regarded as rebutted".

1. **The defendant's attempt to rebut the inference of undue influence that has arisen from proof by the claimant of the existence (actual/presumed) of a relationship of trust and confidence and a transaction which requires explanation**

There's no finite ways in which presumption *can be rebutted*, ways:

1. Showing that the donor acted independently – with appreciation.

2. Showing donor had competent and independent advice

3. Showing donor in making the gift had been a "spontaneous and independent act" *(Re Brocklehurst [1978])*

- Will not suffice to rebut the presumption to show that there was a reasonable explanation for the transaction *(Smith v Cooper [2010])*

Claimant can prove a case of relational undue influence in one of two-ways

1. **He can prove that he reposed trust and confidence in the defendant**

- The defendant abused this trust and confidence.

1. **Or he can prove the existence of a relationship of trust and confidence between himself and the defendant and a transaction that cannot be accounted for on ordinary motives and the evidential burden will then shift to the defendant to rebut the inference of undue influence that has arisen**

— But in both cases, the claimant must show that undue influence has been applied

— In the second case, "the court has drawn appropriate inferences of fact upon a balanced consideration of the whole of the evidence at the end of a trial in which the burden of proof rested upon" the claimant.

10. Performance and Discharge of the Contract

Performance

– Parties enter contracts expecting that it will be performed according to its terms. The contract itself represents a series of terms which determine obligations undertaken by each party.

– Breach of contract results in the innocent party being entitled to a remedy (Photo Production Ltd v Securicor Transport Ltd [1980].

– In many cases, formation and performance of contract is simultaneous. Atiyah offers an example:

– "Obligations are created by what we do, not what we promise or what we intend: in other words it is the payment of the money and handing over of the newspaper which form the basis of the obligations created, not the promise to pay or the promise to hand over the newspaper"

– But in other contracts there may be a time lapse between formation and performance. As such parties promise to undertake obligations to be performed in the future.

– In this case it is the agreement that is the basis of the parties' obligations, and not reliance upon the agreement.

– Even in cases of simultaneous formation and performance, the source of obligation remains the promises from either party.

– Actions can suggest that agreement has been reached in these examples.

Discharge of the Contract

Ways in which contracts can be brought to an end

Discharge by performance

- Occurs when performance of both parties complies fully with the terms of the contract.

- Studying the different aspects of contract law can distort the reality for students – most contracts are discharged by performance.

Discharge by Agreement

- Parties can agree to discharge or abandon/discharge the contract

- Agreement must be supported by consideration.

- Consideration is easy to establish when neither party has performed their obligation since both parties can give up their rights to compel performance of the contract.

- Where a contract is executed on one side, agreement to abandon contract cannot be supported by consideration and will be unenforceable, unless;

1. Agreement is a deed

2. Party who has performed his contract obligations is estopped from going back upon his representation.

3. The party is held to have waived existing rights

- Where one side of a contract is executed an agreement to abandon can itself be supported by fresh consideration.

- A contract could also be discharged by a condition that has been incorporated into the contract – this allows for a contract to be brought to an end on the occurrence of such an event without breach.

Discharge by operation of law

- A contract which is frustrated is ended by the operation of a rule of law. The doctrine of frustration does not look into the intentions or wishes of the parties.

11. Breach of Contract

Introduction: breach defined

— Treitel - "a breach of contract is committed when a party without lawful excuse fails or refuses to perform what is due from him under the contract, or performs defectively or incapacitates himself from performing"

— "Without lawful excuse" is crucial. For example, frustrated contract cannot be breached.

— If a party has right to terminate, and refuses to continue the contract they do not breach.

— Breach can be verbal or through conduct by a contracting party disabling themselves from performing the contract.

— Inability to perform the contract must be proven on the balance of probabilities.

— Difficult to establish when alternative obligations are entered which are inconsistent and not compatible with existing obligations.

— Entering into inconsistent obligations (Alfred C Toepfer International GmbH v Itex Hagrani Export SA (1993) - "does not in itself establish an inability to perform, unless these obligations are of such a nature or have such an effect that it can truly to be said that the party in question has put it out of his power to perform his obligations"

When does breach occur?

— Breach must depend on the terms of each contract.

— Party alleging breach must prove there has been a breach

— Liability does not always depend on proof of fault — strict liability in some contracts.

Section 14 (2) of the Sale of Goods Act 1979 is an example of a *strict contractual obligation:*

1. Seller sells goods, implied condition the goods are of satisfactory quality.

2. Even if seller acts reasonably, if the goods do not reach satisfactory quality he will be in breach.

Liability not always strict...
Section 13 Supply of Goods and Services Act 1982:

— Contract can impose a duty to take reasonable care.

— "A person who supplies a service in the course of a business impliedly undertakes to carry out the service with reasonable care and skill"

The consequences of breach

— Will not automatically end a contract.

— Instead, the innocent party gets various options on how to proceed, these are determined by the seriousness of the breach.

— Even a fundamental breach, does not terminate the contract

Consequence of the breach must be determined on the facts, but *3 principal consequences of breach are identified:*

Damages - Innocent party can get damages for loss from breach

— Can recover damages on proving breach and loss, unless an exclusion clause has been contracted for.

Enforcement by party in breach - Party in breach may be unable to sue to enforce the innocent party's obligations under the contract:

— Party in breach cannot enforce contract against innocent party

— If obligations are independent, breach does not entitle innocent party to abandon performance of contract.

— Ex. Taylor v Webb (1937) - Independent obligations of landlord to repair the premises and tenant's covenant to pay rent (independent). Thys, landlord must carry out repairs even if rent is not provided.

– If dependant then innocent party must be willing and ready to perform his obligations, before he can bring an action against the other party.

– Obligations generally deemed as dependent obligations

– S28 of Sales of Goods Act 1979 - delivery of goods and payment of price are concurrent conditions, in so much as the seller is ready and willing to give possession of goods to buyer in exchange for the price, and buyer must be ready and willing to pay the price in exchange for the possession of goods

Right to terminate the performance of the contract - Breach may entitle innocent party to terminate further performance of the contract:

– Breach of warranty – no right to terminate, damages.

– Breach of condition and breach of innominate term - right to terminate (if consequences serious for IT)

– "Repudiatory breach" - breach giving right to terminate. Also known as 'right to rescind'.

Confusion lies between
"rescission for breach".

– Contract rescinded for breach – set aside prospectively.

– Johnson v Agnew (1980)

– Photo Production Ltd v Securicor Transport Ltd (1980)

"recission for misrepresentation".

– Contract rescinded for misrepresentation - its set aside both retrospectively and prospectively.

– Aim is to put parties in position they would have been if they had never contracted.

– Preferable to avoid confusion between right of the innocent party to terminate further performance, rather than right to rescind

The prospective nature of breach

– Breach operates prospectively

– "right to terminate performance of the contract" more accurate than "right to terminate the contract".

– Contract is not set aside *ab initio*, this is why a contractual term which deals with consequences of a breach is not merely ignored – as it would be if the contract was fully set aside.

– *Primary and secondary obligations* make this clearer.

– *Primary obligation* - obligation to perform contract.

– *Secondary obligation* – obligation create when there is a breach of primary obligation

– Ex. Photo Production Ltd v Securicor Transport Ltd - Lord Diplock, "breaches of primary obligations give rise to substituted secondary obligations"

2 types of secondary obligations:

General secondary obligations

– Primary obligations unchanged.

– Breach creates secondary obligation, imposed upon party in breach

– Secondary obligation to pay damages.

– "to pay monetary compensation to the innocent party for the loss sustained by him in consequence of the breach"

Anticipatory secondary obligation

– Breach of primary obligation allows innocent party to elect to terminate performance of the contract.

– "There is substituted by implication of law for the primary obligations of the party in default which remain unperformed

194

secondary obligation to pay monetary compensation to the other party for the loss sustained by him in consequence of their non-performance"

— Anticipatory secondary obligation assesses damages by looking at the obligations which would have fallen due.

— Lord Diplock wished for ASO to arise in every case of termination, following a breach of condition - Lombard North Central plc v Butterworth (1987)

— In English law, no distinction between condition created by law and condition agreed by parties

The right of election

— Right to terminate performance of contract is a choice.

— Innocent party can also affirm contract.

— Period to decide – reasonableness.

— Can treat it as repudiated if other party persists in his repudiation

— Innocent party has to take reasonable steps to mitigate his loss.

— Must communicate to the party in breach whether or not party wishes to terminate.

— *Lord Steyn (Vitol SA v Norelf (1996)* - requirements for effective acceptance of repudiatory breach:

— "An act of acceptance of repudiation requires no particular form: a communication does not have to be couched in the language of acceptance. It is sufficient that the communication or conduct clearly and unequivocally conveys to the repudiating party that the aggrieved party is treating the conduct as at an end... the aggrieved party need not personally, or by an agent, notify the repudiating party of his election to treat the contract as at an end. It is sufficient that the fact of the election comes to the repudiating party's attention"

— H of L - failure to perform does not constitute acceptance

— Depends "particular contractual relationship and the particular circumstances of the case" whether failure to perform sufficed (Lord Steyn)

— Party choosing to terminate does not have to give the reason for his decision (Arcos Ltd v E A Ronaasen & Son (1933)

— If affirmed, contract still in force and both parties remain bound to perform obligations

— IP who accepts performance of contract after its breach would have affirmed the contract (Davenport v R (1877)

— Affirmation does not stop IP claiming damages suffered due to breach.

— Once contract is terminated, obligations cannot be resurrected (Johnson v Agnew (1980)

Confusion arises as this should not be referred to as a waiver....
Waiver by election

— An innocent contracting dealt a repudiatory breach can terminate or affirm.

— When IP affirms they abandons right to terminate.

Waiver by estoppel

— Waiver is not the abandonment of a right; instead, it is forbearance from exercising a right

— *This is reminiscent of Hughes v Metropolitan Rly Co (1877)*

— When IP unequivocally states to the party in default that he will not use right to terminate

— His conduct also leads the default party in believing that he will not exercise the right

Anticipatory breach

— Definition: a contracting party informs the other party, that prior to deadline for performance, that he will not perform contractual obligations.

196

- Entitles innocent party to terminate immediately.

- Party may be in breach of contract prior to 'breaching contract' under terms of contract (timescale). Seems illogical.

- Rationalisation – there has been a breach. Breach of implied term parties wont repudiate contract prior to performance.

- *Ex. Hochster v De La Tour (1853)* :

- Defendant agreed to employ claimant for 3 months from 1 June

- 11 may - defendant told claimant no longer needed.

- 22 may - claimant commenced action – held this action, and damages, could be claimed successfully now – didn't need to wait.

Innocent party can affirm contract and demand performance from OP at time stipulated in contract.
If IP wants to terminate contract, must give notice to other party - stating acceptance of anticipatory breach.
IP, may continue performance of contract, despite knowledge that performance is not wanted by the other party.
Ex. White and Carter (Councils) Ltd v McGregor (1962)

- Defendant entered into contract with claimant

- Claimant agreed to display adv. of defendant's garage for a period of 3 years on plates attached to litter bins

- On same day, defendants communicated to claimants did not want to perform contract.

- Claimants refused to accept cancellation. Continued performance and sought damages for payment.

- H of L (3/2) - claimants entitled to recover contract price

- Majority (3) - referred to Asquith LJ in *Howard v Pickford Tool Co Ltd (1951)* - "an unaccepted repudiation is a thing writ in water and of no value to anybody"

- Claimants don't have to accept. Unfortunate they "saddled themselves with an unwanted contract causing an apparent waste of time and money"

— Minority - claimants failed to mitigate their loss — not entitled.

— But majority said claimants were not suing for damages — but debt. Rules didn't apply.

Principle of White and Carter

1.

— IP cannot force party in breach to co-operate.

— Where IP cannot perform without co-operation, they will be forced to accept the breach.

— Hounslow LBC v Twickenham Garden Developments Ltd (1971)

2.

— Lord Reid - "if it can be shown that a person has no legitimate interest, financial, or otherwise, in performing the contract rather than claiming damages, he ought not to be allowed to saddle the other party with an additional burden with no benefit to himself"

— The majority (Lord Tucker and Hodson) did not agree

Clea Shipping Corp v Bulk Oil International Ltd (1984)

— Lloyd J - "there comes a point at which the court will cease, on general equitable principles, to allow the IP to enforce his contract according to its strict legal terms"

— No need for IP to act reasonably — in decision over acceptance.

— Party in breach must demonstrate IP had no legitimate interest in completing the contract.

— Defendants in White and Charter — hadn't demonstrated IP had no legitimate interest in completing the contract.

— Must be distinction between *unreasonable*, *wholly unreasonable*, and *perverse* behaviour

- Where IP acts wholly unreasonably (The Odenfield 1978) or perversely (Isabella Shipowner SA v Shaganag Shipping Co Ltd (1912)- court may refuse the IP to continue with performance.

- *wholly unreasonable* – not clear and criticised by Simon J (Ocean Marine Navigation Ltd v Koch Carbon Inc (2003)

Ex. Extreme case - The Alaskan Trader

- Claimants chartered ship to defendants for 24 months

- Post 1 year - ship required extensive repairs

- Defendants said no need for ship.

- But claimants continued to spend £800,000 on extensive repairs.

- When completed kept ship ready as they would have had the defendants wanted to use the ship.

- Arbitrator - claimants acted "wholly unreasonably".

- Appeal upheld by Lloyd J

- Liability of defendants in damages

But decision to affirm contract may work to disadvantage to IP
Disadvantages
1.

- IP who affirms contract could lose rights to sue altogether if contract frustrated between date of unaccepted anticipatory breach and date fixed for performance (Avery v Bowden (1856)

2.

- Where breach not accepted, parties remain subject to their obligations

- Therefore, IP will be liable for pay damages if he fails to accept breach (and breaches contract himself)

12. Obtaining an Adequate Remedy

The entire obligations rule

- Ability of a party to withhold performance under the contract, gives to the other party an incentive to perform his contractual obligations

Example

- Homeowner and construction company contract for a new extension for £8000.

- Under terms payment will be made on the completion of the work to a satisfactory level of quality.

- Payment obligation dependent on building obligation.

- If extension is not completed the construction company cannot sue for payment.

- Any claim barred by the *entire obligations rule ("entire contracts" rule)*

Origin of entire obligations rule

Cutter v Powell (1795)
Facts

- Cutter promised to Powell to "proceed, continue and do his duty as second mate" on a ship sailing from Jamaica to UK.

- Cutter died on the journey.

- Widow sued to recover the wages, she claimed he was owed wages for the period in which he completed promise – i.e. up to his death.

Judgement

- Cutter was not entitled to payment unless the voyage was complete.

— No completion = no payment.

— Powerful incentive to a contracting party to carry out terms.

— But "unjust enrichment" of the innocent party

— *Cutter v Powell* - Powell obtained services of Cutter for seven weeks

— Exceptions can mitigate.

Exceptions to this rule

1. **Rule is alleged not to apply where the party in breach has substantially performed his obligations under the contract** *(Hoenig v Isaacs and Williams v Roffey Bros & Nicholls (Contractors) Ltd [1991])*

— Innocent party must settle for damages for any loss suffered as a result of the breach

— Treitel, "it is based on the error that contracts, as opposed to particular obligations, can be entire".

— "To say that an obligation is entire means that it must be completely performed before payment becomes due" and in relations to entire obligations, there is no scope for any doctrine of "substantial performance".

— Here, the court must identify the obligation which is alleged to be entire

— *Hoenig v Isaacs* - the builder completed the work badly — no need to assess substantiality.

— Obligation which was entire had been performed. Employer had to pay the price, subject to damages for failure to complete work well (non-entire).

— This view has not yet been expressly adopted by the court.

1. **The innocent party may be required to recompense the party in breach if he accepts the latter's part performance**

— Difficult because part performance was requested - full performance or nothing is reality.

Ex. Sumpter v Hedges [1898]

— Half a garage cannot benefit the householder.

— **Court may interpret the contract as consisting of a number of obligations**

— Common. Building contract will often make sure payment is at intervals

— Gives parties scope to mitigate entire obligation rule.

The creation of conditions

— This is an effective remedy - threaten to terminate performance of the contract in the event of a repudiatory breach of contract and claim loss of bargain damages

— Effectiveness seen in case *Lombard North Central plc v Butterworth [1987[*

Facts

— Clause 2 of the agreement – obligation to pay punctually was the essence of the deal.

— Owners could terminate contract and claim damages when hirer did not pay an instalment on time.

Judgement

— COA held that parties could classify a term as a condition. Not subject to rule.

A claim in debt

— **Debt** – sum owed to one party to the contract.

— Distinct from a claim in damages

— Issue is whether or not sum is owed to claimant.

— No need to discuss mitigation of loss or even remoteness.

— no more, no less than sum of debt.

— Advantage of this claim - *White and Charter (Councils) Ltd v McGregor [1962]*

Judgement

— Claimants can reclaim contract price, didn't need to mitigate their loss

— Ability to obtain summary judgement under Part 24 of the Civil Procedure Rules – procedural advantage.

Liquidated damages

— Method where you state the amount of money which shall be payable in the event of a breach of contract

— Removes uncertainty, enables the parties to know potential liability – insurance.

— But the courts have retained a jurisdiction here and can control the terms.

Rules which the courts have established

Liquidated damage clause

— If the clause is a genuine pre-estimate, likely to be enforced.

— If the loss suffered is greater than the sum stipulated, IP can't look beyond clause. *(Diestal v Stevenson [1906])*

— Sum stipulated in the liquidated damages clause is the sum recoverable – this might be bigger or smaller than actual loss.

Penalty clause

— If it is not a genuine pre-estimate, it will likely be deemed a penalty clause.

— Cannot punish.

— Will not be enforced by the court beyond the actual loss of the party seeking to rely on the clause *(Jobson v Johnson [1989])*

Distinction between the clauses

- **intention** of the parties crucial in determining clause.

- 'Genuine' focus can be traced back to decision of H of L in *Dunlop Pneumatic Tyre Co Ltd v New Garage & Motor Co Ltd [1915]*

- **Jackson J** *(Alfred McAlpine Capital Projects Ltd v Tilebox Ltd [2005])* - substituted the word "reasonable" for "genuine".

- This change in emphasis is important

- The focus of genuineness is on parties' intention. Link to reasonableness; i.e., the more unreasonable the clause, the less likely to have been genuine.

- Looking for a "substantial discrepancy" between the clause and loss likely to be suffered – this is how to find penalty.

Rules of construction which they apply in deciding whether a particular clause is a penalty clause

- **Lord Dunedin** *(Dunlop Pneumatic Tyre Co Ltd v New Garage & Motor Co Ltd [1915])*

Clause will be held to be a penalty clause... if

- Extravagant and unconscionable compared to greatest conceivable loss.

- If the breach is not making payment, and the sum provided is sum greater than the sum which was initially demanded.

- There is a presumption that it is penalty when "a single lump sum is made payable by way of compensation, on the occurrence of one or more or all of several events, some of which may occasion serious and others but trifling damage".

Fourth rule

- If impossible to estimate loss – doesn't make it a penalty.

Courts will operate especially carefully when contracting parties are commercially aware:

Ex. Phillips Hong Kong Ltd v A-G of Hong Kong (1993)

- **Lord Woolfe** - recognised the value of agreed clauses in enabling the parties "know with a reasonable degree of certainty the extent of their liability and the risks which they run as a result of entering into the contract".

- Penalty clause jurisdiction is exceptional : "the principle was always recognised as being subject to fairly narrow constraints, and the courts have always avoided claiming that they have any general jurisdiction to rewrite the contracts that the parties have made".

- "The court should not be too ready to find the requisite degree of disproportion lest they impinge on the parties' freedom to settle for themselves the rights and liabilities following a breach of contract" *(Mason and Wilson JJ in High Court of Australia in AMEV UDC Finance Ltd v Austin (1986))*

- Argument considered in *Phillips* - sum claimed was not exorbitant. However, due to what actually happened the clause was nevertheless a penalty clause because there were various hypothetical situations in which the application of the clause could have resulted in a sum larger than the actual loss being recovered by the innocent party.

Privy Council rejected this argument:

- "Except possibly in the case of situations where one of the parties to the contract is able to dominate the other as to the choice of the terms of a contract, it will normally be insufficient to establish that a provision is objectionably penal to identify situations where the application of the provision could result in a larger sum being recovered by the injured party than his actual loss. Even in such situations so long as the sum payable in the event of non-compliance with the contract is not extravagant, having regard to the range of losses that it could reasonably be anticipated it would have to cover at the time the contract was made, it can still be a genuine pre-estimate of the loss that would be suffered and so a perfectly valid liquidated damage provision. The use in argument of unlikely illustrations should therefore not assist a party to defeat a provision as to liquidated damages".

205

- Focus has to be on time of formulation.

- But as Lord Woolf stated, not to say what happens post-formulation is not relevant.

- What happened "can provide valuable evidence as to what could reasonably be expected to be the loss at the time the contract was made".

- Courts seem to be reluctant to setting aside an agreed pre-estimation of loss by parties of equal bargaining power

- Clause may only consider one party.

Ex. Cine Bes Filmcilik ve Yapimcilik v United International Pictures [2003]

- CO A - a clause in a licensing agreement could be penal because it made provision for various payments to be made by the licensee to the licensor on the termination of the agreement without giving credit to licensee.

- But this approach not always followed – more relaxed approach:

Ex. Murray v Leisureplay plc [2005]
Facts

- Contract of employment said, "in the event of wrongful termination by way of liquidated damages the company shall forthwith pay to the Executive a sum equal to one year's gross salary, pension contributions, and other benefits in kind".

Judgement

- The clause was penal; it failed to take account of the executive's obligation to mitigate his loss by looking for alternative employment following the termination of his contract

- COA - recognised that the clause was generous, but nevertheless held that the clause was enforceable as a liquidated damages clause

- Thus, overcompensation will not inevitably lead to penal.

- In *Murray*, COA drew distinction between clause which was **"generous" (enforceable)** and a clause which was **"extravagant or unconscionable" (not enforceable)**

- Penalty clause = invalid and not enforceable.

- Creation of anomaly that loss innocent party has suffered is greater than the sum stipulated in the contract

- In such a case, can the innocent party argue that the clause is a penalty clause, so they can ignore it and actually claim via normal damages route?

Ex. Wall v Rederiaktiebogalet Luggude [1915]

- Held that innocent party can argue this and recover his actual loss

- However, the decision was only at first instance.

- Liquated damages clause can be valid even if they provide for less than estimate of loss. *(Cellulose Acetate Silk Co v Widnes Foundry (1925)*

- IF clause is held to "exclude or restrict" liability for breach of contract, it may be caught by the Unfair Contract Terms Act 1977

Evading the penalty clause rule

- Privy Council in *Phillips Hong Kong Ltd v A-G of Hong Kong*, may suggest that parties will in the future have greater latitude in making provision for agreed damages in the contract itself

Three principal devices can be used to avoid the rule

1. **Penalty clause rule does not apply if a clause only accelerates an existing liability**

- Not caught by the penalty clause rule *(Protector Loan Co v Grice (1880))*

- Crucial ingredient in these cases — must be "present debt, which by reason of an indulgence given by the creditor is payable either in the future or in a lesser amount, provided that certain conditions are met" *(O'Dea v Allstates Leasing System (WA) Pty Ltd (1983))*

1. To stipulate that the sum shall be payable on an event which is not a breach of contract

– Rule applies only to sums of money which are payable on a breach of contract *(Euro London Appointments Ltd v Claessens International Ltd [2006])*

– Potential evasion shown in *Alder v Moore [1961]*

Facts

– Defendant (professional footballer) suffered serious injury and was certified as being disabled.

– Claimant insurers paid him £500 under an insurance policy.

– Policy undertaken to cover the defendant in the event of his suffering permanent total disablement

– defendant covenanted with claimants that:

– *"In consideration of the above payment i hereby declare and agree that I will take no part as a playing member of any form of professional football and that in the event of infringement of this condition I will be subject to a penalty of [£500]"*

– Defendant later resumed his playing career – insurers sought to get money back.

– Defendant argued it was a penalty clause.

Judgement

– COA - held that the penalty clause rule was not applicable

– Defendant had not promised to never play again.

– Hence, £500 was not payable upon a breach of contract and the penalty clause rule was irrelevant

– Penalty clause rule can lead to *anomalous results*

– Hirer in breach of hire-purchase can invoke the penalty clause rule if the owners try to recover an "excessive" sum of money for breach.

– But if the hirer honestly admits that he can no longer pay the instalments, returns the goods, the hirer will have no defence to an action by the owners for an "excessive" sum of money. (*Bridge v Campbell Discount Co Ltd [1962]*)

– Lord Denning emphasised that this rule does not make sense - "absurd paradox" that "it will grant relief to a man who breaks his contract but will penalise the man who keeps it".

1. **To avoid the use of a clause which states that a specified sum of money shall be payable in the event of a breach of contract because there is always a risk that such clause will be held to be a penalty clause**

– However, if the parties state the term is a condition, breach of that term will allow the innocent party to terminate performance and claim damages

– Disadvantage – doesn't attempt to quantify the loss; therefore it doesn't obtain the procedural advantages which accompany a claim for a liquidated sum.

– This means claimant has to prove loss in normal method.

Deposits and part payments

– Clause stating certain sum to be paid on breach = risky, could be found penalty.

– Innocent party must take the initiative to obtain the money

– Might be preferred to obtain payment of a sum of money in advance, and then not return it if there was a breach.

– But in such a case, can the party in breach recover the payment?

Depends if deposit or part payment.

– **Deposit** – security, and is generally irrevocable

- **Part Payment** normally recoverable, part of contract payment.

- construction key

- If contract is **neutral** – any payment is usually treated as a part payment *(Dies v British and International Mining and Finance Co [1939])*

- *Howe v Smith (1884)* - a deposit is irrevocable

- Deposit which was due prior to discharge, but which has not been paid is forfeitable *(Hinton v Sparkes (1868))*

- Rule causes hardship to the party in breach if deposit larger than the loss resulting from breach

Limit on ability of parties to demand excessive deposit established by the privy council in *Workers Trust and Merchant Bank Ltd v Dojap Investments Ltd [1993]*

Facts

- Sellers of property tried to forfeit a deposit of 25% purchase price after a purchaser failed to pay the purchase price within the 14 days – this timing was at the root of the contract.

- Purchasers did pay purchase price with interest a week later but the vendors refused the cheque and purported to forfeit the deposit of almost 3 million Jamaican dollars.

Judgement

- Held sellers could not retain the deposit and ordered that it be repaid to the purchasers

- **Lord Browne-Wilkinson** - "it was not possible for the parties to attach the incidents of a deposit to the payment of a sum of money unless such sum is reasonable as earnest money"

- Tricky to determine "a reasonable deposit", given that a reasonable deposit need not represent a genuine pre-estimate of the loss.

- Held that the customary deposit in the case of the sale of land has been 10% and that a "vendor who seeks to obtain a larger amount must show special circumstances which justify such a deposit"

— Sellers here could not justify.

— Privy Council 10% deposit was "Without logic", still decided to use it as a benchmark

— Not clear how reasonable will just judged without some kind of objective benchmark.

Difficult aspects of the case

1. **Do courts have jurisdiction to relieve against the forfeiture of the deposit even when party is not ready and willing to perform contract.**

— **Romer LJ** *(Stockloser v Johnson [1954])* - the jurisdiction of the court was confined to permitting late completion by the defaulting party.

— **Denning and Somervell LJJ** — jurisdiction if it was unconscionable for the innocent party to retain the money.

— Forfeiture of a 25% deposit was a "plain penalty" - *Comr of Public Works v Hills [1906*

1. **In the event of a deposit being held to be unreasonable, court won't redraw contract to include a reasonable deposit**

— Sellers could retain 10% of the sum paid as they had not contracted for a 10% deposit

— Refusal to rewrite terms of the contract will give an incentive to contracting parties to err on the side of caution when setting the level of any deposit payable

— *Dojap* - limits upon liability of the contracting parties to provide for excessive deposits

Limits of Dojap

1. **Only concerned with the right of the innocent party to retain the deposit**

2. **It doesn't try to restrict the right of the innocent party to terminate the contract**

Ex. Union Eagle Ltd v Golden Achievement Ltd [1997]

Facts

- The claimant agreed to buy a flat in Hong Kong and paid 10% of the purchase price for a deposit.

- Agreement referred to date, time and place. The time was specifically noted as being the essence of the contract.

- Completion required by 30 September 1991 (prior to 5pm on that day)

- Clause 12 - if the purchaser failed to adhere to terms and conditions of the agreement, the seller was given right to rescind the contract and forfeit the deposit

- Claimant failed to complete by the stipulated time – ten mins late.

- Sellers did not accept late payment, rescinded the contract and forfeited the deposit

- Claimant sought to have the contract enforced.

Judgement

- His action failed

- Privy Council rejected his argument of unconscionability.

- PC rejected – it was contrary to the authorities and to the needs of the business world

- **Lord Hoffmann** – focussed on need for certainty in commercial transactions.

- Law should allow vendor to know whether or not he could terminate

- Mitigation of rule - **possibility** that a court will *give a personal restitutionary claim to the purchaser where a seller is unjustly enriched of work done or payment prior to termination.*

– Approach is that, while a vendor should have restored to him the "freedom to deal with his land as he pleases"; should not get such freedom in relation to money paid to him.

– Exceptional cases where **equity will intervene** to prevent a party from exercising his right to terminate; if estopped.

– Equity intervention for mortgage or rent due under a lease *(G and C Kreglinger v New Patagonia Meat and Cold Storage Co Ltd [1914])*

Where sum is interpreted as **part payment, sum is recoverable by the party in breach**

– Rule in *Dies*

Facts

– Claimant contracted to purchase ammunition, including pre-payment of £100,000

– Claimant refused to accept delivery, in breach.

– Defendants terminated the contract and the claimant sued to recover £100,000

Judgement

– **Stable J** – claimant could recover the money paid.

– This right was subject to right of the defendants to recover damages for breach

– Pre-payment was conditional upon subsequent performance of the contract – when condition was not met the defendant's right to retain the money simultaneously failed

But rule in *Dies* was re-examined by H of L in - *Hyundai Shipbuilding and Heavy Industries Co Ltd v Papadopoulos [1980]*
Facts

– Shipbuilders sought to recover an instalment which they alleged was owed to them by the defendant guarantors

Judgement

- Held that shipbuilders could recover.

- **Lord Fraser** - distinguished *Dies* because the latter case was not one where sellers were required to incur any expenditure or perform any work in the performance of their obligations under the contract.

- This was just a simple contract.

- *Hyundai* , involved a contract for work and materials – builders incurred costs.

Liquidated damages, penalty clauses, and forfeitures: an assessment

- **Why should we differentiate between penalty clauses and deposits?**

- After *Workers Trust and Merchant Bank Ltd v Dojap Investments Ltd* , we don't now need to distinguish between the 2:

- Penalty clause is simply applied to deposits *(UK Housing Alliance (North West) Ltd v Francis [2010])*, where Longmore LJ said the PC in Dojap, had "Applied the law relating to penalties since the sum was payable on breach".

- Penalty clause vs liquidated damages clause – depends on "genuine pre-estimate of the loss".

- Deposits- the crucial question is whether the deposit is "reasonable"?

- Lord Browne-Wilkinson has argued that, for contract for the sale of land, a deposit could be "reasonable" despite not a genuine pre-estimate of the loss.

- "genuine re-estimate of loss" doesn't apply to deposits

- Lord Browne-Wilkinson's argument confined to contracts for the sale of land.

Difference between agreed damages clause and a deposit is that...

- **Deposit** - is payable in advance – it belongs to the recipient before the breach

- **Agreed damages** - only becomes payable when there is a breach

Consequences

- **Deposit** – recipient of deposit less likely than the intended recipient of a sum of agreed damages to have to engage in litigation to obtain the sum stipulated

Due to the tendency of damages to undercompensate; many arguments can be made for leaving the parties free decide damages payable upon a breach

Arguments in favour:

1. **Freedom of contract**

2. **Artificiality of the present rules**

3. **Increase certainty**

Arguments against:
Courts should determine compensation;

- *Main objection* - the courts would have to create a doctrine of unconscionability to step into role of equitable consideration.

- general doctrine of unconscionability has been rejected *(National Westminster Bank v Morgan [1985])*

- case for a general doctrine is strengthened by **Unfair Terms in Consumer Contracts Regulations 1999**

- It includes within the list of **terms** (which are indicatively unfair) the following terms, which overlap with the existing common law regulation of penalty clauses and deposits *(Office of Fair Trading v Abbey National plc [2008])*

Terms
Term which has the object or effect of:

1. *"Permitting the seller or supplier to retain sums paid by the consumer where the latter decides not to conclude or perform the contract, without providing for the consumer to receive compensation of an equivalent amount from the seller or supplier where the latter is the party cancelling the contract" (Schedule 2, paragraph 1(d))*

   – This deals with deposits which is in a manner unfamiliar to English lawyers

   – **Treitel -** this provision rests on "the civil law institution by which a contract can, in effect, be dissolved on forfeiture of a deposit or on the return by the payee of double amount".

1. *"Requiring any consumer who fails to fulfil his obligation to pay a disproportionately high sum in compensation" (Schedule 2, paragraph 1(e))*

   – Word "disproportionately" not defined. Not clear what is meant by "fails to fulfil his obligation".

Advantages of the provisions

   – Avoid artificiality of current rules.

   – Also reduce ability of clever draftsmanship.

Specific performance

   – Claimant may seek specific performance.

   – Order of **Specific performance** – orders parties to carry out obligations.

   – This protects expectation interest.

   – Equitable remedy which is only available in the discretion of the court

   – Only really available where damages are inadequate.

   – Gradual expansion in recent years

Ex. Beswick v Beswick [1968]

   – H of L envisaged a wider role for specific performance

– This wider role: appropriateness of remedies, not hierarchy of remedies.

– **Lord Reid** - awarded specific performance to achieve a "just result"

– **Lord Pearce** – if it was "the more appropriate remedy"

– *Beswick* - there is now "a right to specific performance of all contracts where there is no adequate reason for the courts to refuse it" (Lawson)

– Treitel, "the availability of specific performance depends on the appropriateness of that remedy in the circumstances of each case".

Situations in which an order of specific performance is not available

Remedy is unavailable where...

1. Would cause severe hardship to the defendant *(Patel v Ali [1984])*

2. Contract unfair to the defendant, but not enough to set aside. *(Walters v Morgan (1861))*

3. Claimant's conduct demonstrates that he does not deserve the remedy *(Shell UK Ltd v Lostock Garages Ltd [1976])*

4. Mistake by the defendant which the claimant is trying to take advantage of. *(Webster v Cecil (1861)*

5. Performance impossible *(Watts v Spence [1976])*

6. Personal service contract *(i.e. a contract of employment) (Trade Union and Labour Resolutions/Consolidation Act 1992, s 236)*

7. Vagueness *(Tito v Waddell [1977])*

– Court "Will not compel a defendant to perform his obligations specifically if it cannot at the same time ensure that any unperformed obligations of the [claimant] will be specifically performed, unless perhaps damages would be an adequate remedy for any default on the [claimant's] part" *(Price v Strange [1978])* Uncertainty?

– *Ex. Hill v C A Parsons Ltd [1972]*

– *Ex. Irani v Southampton AHA [1985]*

– Courts were prepared specifically to enforce a contract of employment.

– Increased willingness to grant orders of specific performance

This can be questioned in HoL:
Co-operative Insurance Society Ltd v Argyll Stores (Holdings) Ltd [1998]
Facts

– Claimants were freehold owners of a shopping centre – let a unit to defendants for purpose of running a supermarket.

– 35 years from 1979 and defendants promised to "keep open the demised premises for retail trade" for whole time.

– 1995 - the defendants decided to close store after heavy losses.

– Stripped store out.

– Claimants sought specific performance.

Judgement

– Trial judge refused to grant the order

– COA (majority) granted the order

2 factors drove majority of the COA

1. Claimants would have had serious difficulty in proving the loss which they had suffered due to the breach

2. The defendants conducted themselves with "unmitigated commercial cynicism"

House of Lord's Judgement

– H of L allowed the defendants' appeal:

Their conclusion was relied on a number of factor...

1. Settle rule not to force defendant to run a business.

2. could expose defendant to enormous losses

3. What was meant by keeping it running? One item on shelf?

4. It was oppressive

5. No public interest in requiring someone to carry on a business at a loss

"Sound sense" to refuse. The trial judge had acted within his discretion.

Criticism

— Too much focus on defendant?

— Shouldn't focus be on claimant – adequacy?

Can the parties contract for an order of specific performance?

Ex. Quadrant Visual Communications Ltd v Hutchison Telephone UK Ltd [1993]

— **Stocker LJ** - "once the court is asked for the equitable remedy of specific performance, its discretion cannot be fettered" by stipulation of the parties

— Parties couldn't confine courts to "rubber stamp" role.

— In this case, there was trickery.

— Therefore, easy to understand why the court paid little or no attention to any agreed stipulation for specific performance

— However, in other contexts, where there is no "wrongdoing" by claimant. The stipulation should be a factor which is taken into account by the court in the exercise of its discretion (*Warner Bros Pictures Inc v Nelson [1937]*)

Civil vs English system:

Article 9-102 of the Principles of European Contract Law

1. The aggrieved party is entitled to specific performance of an obligation other than one to pay money, including the remedying of a defective performance

2. Specific performance cannot, however, be obtained where:

(a) performance would be unlawful or impossible; or
(b) performance would cause the debtor unreasonable effort or expense; or
(c) the performance consists in the provision of services or work of a personal character or depends upon a personal relationship; or
(d) the aggrieved party may reasonably obtain performance from another source

1. The aggrieved party will lose the right to specific performance if it fails to seek it within a reasonable time after it has or ought to have become aware of the non-performance

- The factors listed in P2 relate to those which would be considered by an English court.

- Difference between the systems (2) is ultimately one which concerns the location of the burden of proof

- *English law* - burden is on the claimant -show appropriateness.

- *Civilian system* – for the defendant to prove otherwise.

- **But Should English courts adopt this more expansive approach found in civilian systems?**

- **Should SP be generally available?**

- Can be argued that damages under compensate.

- The fact a claimant even asks for specific performance indicate they do not believe damages are adequate.

- Often, claimants have an incentive to not try for specific performance

- Claimants' might want to purchase alternative goods in the marketplace, and then sue for damages, as opposed to waiting for a court to make an order of specific performance

Arguments against such proposition

1. **Need limitations where contracts involve personal or intimate relations and in cases where it would be impossi-**

ble for the court to supervise the order because of the vagueness inherent in the contract

— It shouldn't be assumed that an order of specific performance will always lead to the performance of the contract

— Gives claimant a choice

Claimant can:

1. Insist upon performance

2. He can sell the right to the defendant

— Defendant may then be forced to negotiate his way out of the contract with the claimant

Injunctions

— Breach of a negative contract can be strained by means of an injunction

— **Injunction** - is also an equitable remedy.

— Injunction won't be given granted where its effect would be directly or indirectly to compel the defendant to perform acts which would not be compelled by SP

— Injunctions used in trade cases to stop the employee or vendor acting in breach of agreement. Not confined to trade…

Ex. Araci v Fallon [2011]
Facts

— Race-horse owner obtained an interim injunction to restrain a defendant jockey from riding another horse in the Derby – in breach of covenant.

— Retainer agreement.

— In breach, the defendant sought to ride a different horse in the Derby

Judgement

— COA - granted injunctive relief to the claimant to restrain the defendant from riding other horse

— In doing so, the COA attached importance to the fact that the defendant was seeking to act in **flagrant breach** of a contract into which he had entered voluntarily – damages would not be adequate.

Damages in lieu of specific performance

— High Court has a discretion to award a claimant damages in lieu of an injunction or specific performance (Senior Courts Act 1981, s 50)

— Where court awards damages, these are assessed on the same basis as common law damages for breach of contract *(Johnson v Agnew [1980]);cf Surrey CC v Bredero Homes Ltd [1993])*

Conclusion
Points to note

1. **Scope for parties to determine own remedies on a breach of contract**

— restrictions can be evaded by careful draftsmanship

— Not true that law of contract resembles the law of tort

— In many cases, remedies do rest upon the agreement of the parties

1. **The "interests "which the law of contract seeks to protect**

— Law of contract seeks to protect the expectation interest.

— Distinguishes law of contract from the law of tort and law of restitution

1. **Law of contract is not always committed to the protection of the expectation interest**

— Supplementary policies - mitigation and remoteness.

— Cautious application of specific performance.

– committed to the protection of individual autonomy and the protection of the expectation interest

– Weight against considerations of fairness, consumerism, and altruism

About the Author

Mohammed Subhan Hussain is an author and active contributing member at King's College London. He has previously published a research paper titled, 'A Momentary Glimpse of the Moon of Bliss: A Conceptual Framework of Justice within the Semantic Tapestries of Legal Pluralism' in The Dickson Poon Transnational Law Institute, King's College London Research Paper Series. He is also the recipient of a full merit-based scholarship at BPP University Law School with experience in legal research, analysis, writing, and reviewing.

If you enjoyed this book, please consider leaving an online review. The author would appreciate reading your thoughts.

Follow Sulis International Press
Subscribe to the newsletter: https://sulisinternational.com/subscribe/

Follow us:
https://www.facebook.com/SulisInternational
https://twitter.com/Sulis_Intl
https://www.pinterest.com/Sulis_Intl/
https://www.instagram.com/sulis_international/

www.ingramcontent.com/pod-product-compliance
Lightning Source LLC
Chambersburg PA
CBHW031848200326
41597CB00012B/315